BEING
BEING HAPPY
BEING GAY

Pathways to a Rewarding Life for Lesbians and Gay Men

BEING
BEING HAPPY
BEING GAY

Pathways to a Rewarding Life for Lesbians and Gay Men

Bert Herrman

ALAMO SQUARE PRESS
SAN FRANCISCO

BEING • BEING HAPPY • BEING GAY. Copyright © 1990 by Bert Herrman. All rights reserved. Printed in the United States of America. No part of this book may be used or reproduced in any manner whatsoever without permission except in the case of brief quotations embodied in critical articles or reviews. For information, address Alamo Square Press, P.O Box 14543, San Francisco, CA 94114.

Quotation from *Society and the Healthy Homosexual* by George Weinberg © 1972 by St. Martin's Press. Reprinted by permission of the publisher.

Quotation from *The Homosexual Matrix* by C.A. Tripp © 1975 by McGraw-Hill. Reprinted by permission of the publisher.

Quotation from *Motivation and Personality* by Abraham Maslow © 1954 by Harper & Row. Reprinted by permission of the publisher.

Library of Congress Catalog Card Number: 89-81744

ISBN: 0-9624751-0-6

TO MY MOTHER
who has loved me through everything.

Acknowledgements

Special thanks to Celeste West, Alan Goodman, Mary Midgett, Dr. Michael Bettinger, N.A. Diaman, wise counsel Jerry Bakken, copy editor Karen Schiller and dozens of others who helped bring this book from dream to reality.

Table of Contents

Introduction	9
Chapter 1. The Psychology of Being	13
Your Authentic Self	13
Programming	14
Self-Esteem	15
Egotism and Self-Hate	16
Commitment	17
Love	18
Happiness	20
Chapter 2. Lesbian/Gay Lifestyles	25
Tom	26
Beth	30
Randy	33
Sky	35
Aleatha	37
Charles	38
Bud	41
Monty	43
Carl	45
Chapter 3. Secular Philosophies	49
Juan	49
Phil	51
Rita	54
Chapter 4. Spiritual Paths	57
Christianity	58
Maxine	60
Judaism	62
Jonathon	64
The Social Responsibility Faiths	65

Anthony	66
Eastern Religion	67
Buddhism	68
Rachel	70
Krishna Consciousness	73
Yoga	74
Paganism	75
Helena	76
Generic Spirituality	78
Felix	79
Mysticism	81
Gloria	83
Chapter 5. Developing Your Unique Self	**89**
Self-Exploration	90
Values Clarification	91
Values Assessment	92
Overcoming Judgment	94
Centering	96
Willingness	97
Forgiveness	97
Meditation	98
Affirmations	100
Visualizations	102
Seeking Professional Help	102
Anne	104
Finding Love and Community	106
Maximizing Your Energy	109
Experimenting	110
Moving On	111
Getting Started	113
Appendix	**117**
Notes	**121**
For Further Reading	**123**

"O father, O mother, O wife, O brother, O friend, I have lived with you after appearances hitherto. Henceforward I am the truth's . . . I must be myself. I cannot break myself any longer for you, or you. If you can love me for what I am, we shall be the happier. If you cannot, I will still seek to deserve that you should. I will not hide my tastes or aversions. I will so trust that what is deep is holy, that I will do strongly before the sun and moon whatever only rejoices me and the heart appoints. If you are noble, I will love you; if you are not, I will not hurt you and myself with hypocritical attentions. If you are true, but not in the same truth with me, cleave to your companions; I will seek my own. I do this not selfishly but humbly and truly. It is alike your interest and mine, and all men's, however long we have dwelt in lies, to live in truth."

                                                Ralph Waldo Emerson
                                                "Self Reliance"

Introduction

Twenty years ago, when I first accepted the fact that I was gay, I didn't know what it would mean. I was doing graduate work in journalism after a degree in business. On the rebound from a woman "who done me wrong," I was agreeably seduced by the handsome, though flaming, leading man of the campus theater group. I have ever since had a warm spot in my heart for redheads.

In the service, I was stationed in Washington, D.C., where I had the free time to cruise the streets of Georgetown one day and spend the next rapping with hippies in Dupont Circle or studying in a Christian Science reading room. I was enthralled with Nichiren Shoshu Buddhism and began chanting in earnest several times a day.

As a desk soldier in Vietnam, I stretched further past my Jewish roots and began attending Protestant services where I sensed a source of strength which enabled me to rise above the demoralizing aspects of the war. My sexual expression was essentially put on hold. For gay soldiers in time of war, discretion may have been the hardest part of valor.

After the service, I assumed my planned career in corporate public relations, while stalking the gay bars of Philadelphia by night, seeking men. I became involved with intellectualized, social responsibility religion and was fortunate to find a straight community that cared more about my integrity than my sexual preference. I lived a triple life—stressful but satisfying.

I was an activist—rallying for peace, organizing for abortion rights, tutoring ghetto youngsters and coordinating a food co-op. I helped found the city's gay political organization.

After fifteen driven years, trying to prove to myself and those around me that I was okay even though I was gay, I walked away from an 8-year relationship with a doctor and a publishing business that had also gone down the tubes. I was burned out on social action. I wandered off to sunny Fort Lauderdale, to ponder the meaning of life and pick up a good tan.

I began reading and studying with an enthusiasm I had never found in college, devouring about five books a week, burying myself in psychology and Eastern religion.

When I felt I'd finished with every worthwhile book in the Fort Lauderdale public library and most of the interesting men in the city, I moved to San Francisco to continue the extensive research leading to this book.

A book such as this could not have been written twenty years ago, although many of the psychological insights come from the humanist psychology, feminist and human potential movements that had already begun to blossom at that time. Gay liberation and its eventual offshoot, gay self-esteem, only began to take hold in the aftermath of the Stonewall riots of 1969. Until that time, if you were gay and your life was going well, you had the good sense to keep your shades drawn. You knew with certainty that the outside world was just waiting to invade with hatchets and crowbars to destroy your house of cards. That's how it was when I first came out.

It took many years for me to discover who I was, to find peace of mind and a life I really find joyous. It meant a great deal of searching, much of it in nooks and crevices where most people never look. This book is a collection of my findings and the experiences of other gay men and women who have each taken their own journey.

It is sad that in 1990 it is almost politically incorrect to admit to being a gay man and happy. Watching so many friends wrestling and succumbing to AIDS is a severe test. It is now, more than ever, essential that we begin staking out the positive territory of being gay and being ourselves.

Gays are one of the few oppressed minorities who continuously regenerate themselves from the general population. Each day, thousands of lesbians and gay men are uncovering their natural tendencies and taking their first crucial step toward self-discovery. It is my hope that some of the many grappling with the rigors of gay life will find encouragement from this book, shoot for the moon, and maybe just make it.

Introduction

A rich and rewarding life is every person's right as a human being. For hundreds of years, lesbians and gay men have bought into the myth that we are somehow inferior and not entitled. The time has come to trash that myth, to acknowledge that an ever-increasing number of gay people are each day crossing the threshold of self-fulfillment.

Our challenges and options are in some ways different from those faced by people who identify themselves as heterosexual. But in the final analysis, every individual, straight or gay, who reaches the higher strata of well-being does it because she or he has the courage to reach beyond the mediocre and the "acceptable," to strive for and fulfill their authentic nature as a unique human being.

"Being gay means having freed oneself of misgivings over being homosexual. At its best it means not limiting oneself to a stereotype—a model of some previous homosexual—for one's personality, at work, at parties, with a lover. It means remaining free to invent, to imbue life with fantasy. It means being able to investigate one's preferences and desires in sexual roles where one chooses, without having to construct a personality elsewhere consistent with this, to justify it, to account for it. In essence, it means being convinced that any erotic preference may be housed in any human being."

                      Dr. George Weinberg
                      Society and the Healthy Homosexual[1]

Chapter 1.
The Psychology of Being

Your Authentic Self

The word is out. "*You* are perfect." Each of us has the potential within us to be one perfect example of ourself. We are each a unique creation, as different as every snowflake. Your combination of chromosomes never existed before anywhere. As an acorn is meant to become an oak tree, you are meant to become you. Studies of identical twins separated at childhood reveal just how much was pre-established in their genetic coding.

You have no need to be anyone except who you are, and you really can't be anyone else, even if you try. You are not Eleanor Roosevelt, Dag Hammarskjold or Christopher Isherwood. None of us are the brothers and sisters to whom our parents compared us, nor are we the Joneses with whom we have wasted so much time trying to keep pace.

Since you were a small child, you knew you were different from others. You could draw a little better, or a little less well. You could not run as fast as other children, or you could run faster. You discovered you were drawn physically to members of your own sex as well as, or instead of, the other sex. You were born with some traits and abilities; others developed along the way. It's difficult to know which are which.

Remember how, even as a child, you wanted to be called by your own name. You wanted your own birthday. As you grew up, you tried to discover your own personality and at some time or other at least peeked at your horoscope to see if it revealed the real you.

Certainly we are not at this moment everything we have the

potential to be, but the joy of living is the active process of fulfilling this potential, developing that which is already within us. But are we realizing this happiness?

Somewhere along the way most of us have gotten lost. We find life bitter and unrewarding. What happened? Where did we go wrong?

Programming

Whether an acorn successfully becomes an oak tree depends on soil, weather and a thousand other variables. So it goes with us as well. Parents begin programming us at infancy. As they provide shelter and sustenance, they attempt to train us in the skills we will need to make it through life. They share with us their knowledge and their ignorance as well.

Our parents teach us what they see as right and wrong behavior, how to survive and how to succeed. To the degree that the knowledge is suitable for who we are and for reality as we will know it, the training is helpful. To the degree that the knowledge is self-serving for them and counter-productive to us, it will confuse us and make our trials more difficult.

As our parents judge our value, so will develop the roots of our self-esteem, our respect for our own uniqueness. If they discourage our self-respect and bend us in ways unnatural to us, they will plant the seeds of hostility and mental illness as we strive vainly to be something we are not.

From our earliest childhood, life is a constant confrontation between what we want or think we want, and that which is expected and acceptable. While school may be a necessary evil, as it exists it is a part of a complex system of authority and regimentation that succeeds in robbing many children of the will to strive for their authentic selves. We are trained to find an acceptable job, join acceptable groups, marry an acceptable spouse and have the acceptable number of children.

Our teachers, our classmates and the television set stress the importance of conformity. If we are offered a choice between consumer values and some religious faith, we are confused. Even religious values come to us in preprocessed form, eternal truths, quick-frozen for convenience, rather than living guidelines for individual growth.

Some fortunate people are able to adapt their authentic selves to fit within the available system; some successfully rebel and reach out in other directions; most lose their vitality along the way and never realize it's gone.

Psychologist Rollo May explains how neurosis is essentially our unused potentialities, blocked by hostile external conditions and internal conflicts, which turn inward on us to destroy rather than create.[2]

It's certainly no wonder that homosexuals were branded neurotic for so many years. What's surprising is that so many lesbians and gay men have been able to accomplish as much as we have, considering the negative conditioning.

Self-Esteem

Maturity, self-respect, self-esteem—they all are based on the ability to know ourselves and spend our time and energies fulfilling values that are meaningful to us. When our living is tuned in to our authentic selves we have the opportunity for *being*. This does not mean merely existing. *Being* means living in the here and now, this moment. It means finding joy and satisfaction in life even through the gravest difficulties. It means taking pleasure in being alive and in our accomplishments even if nobody knows about them but us.

Being is the hallmark of self-esteem. We can recollect the past; we can anticipate the future; but the moment of enjoyment is only in the present. Life speeds by and can only be appreciated this second, the next and the next after that. If we are true to ourselves, we will continually find joy in the process of living. We will recognize beauty in expected and unexpected places. We will be happy that our glass is half full instead of pitying ourselves that it is half empty.

It is the great bugaboo of humankind to concentrate on the value of life and ignore the importance of living. Training ourselves to make the most of *this second* requires discipline. We must pay attention. Life is never going to come; it's here and it's not coming back. Every flower that we pass holds the essence of the joy of this second. This is the meaning of "wake up and smell the roses."

People with low self-esteem try vainly to exist in the past or future—sorting over past accomplishments, remembering the good old days or fantasizing in their dreams. "Wait until I finish school, then I'll be happy." "Wait until I find someone to love, then I'll be happy." "Wait until I get a raise (or retire from this awful job), then I'll be happy." Retirees wonder how they let the best parts of their lives slip away—planting rose bushes after they've lost their sense of smell.

It is not easy to make one's life fit together meaningfully. We let society press us into social situations that bring little satisfaction, and into work niches that are hollow, meaningless and leading nowhere. We think maturity is a matter of age instead of a measure of wisdom and self-control.

Maturity is integrated living, directed toward self-chosen goals. It requires knowing what one wants and why, not simply like a child wants candy because other children want it. A mature person works not from automatic routine, but with conscious belief in the value of the labor.

The mature person is not riddled with anxiety, because mature people have confidence in where they are going. The philosopher Kierkegaard defined anxiety as the "fear of non-being." By this he meant not only the fear of death, but the *fear of life* without meaningful direction, bottled-up energy, festering without a creative, positive outlet.

Anxiety indicates an absence of purpose, the inability to relax, be and enjoy. It's not surprising that ours has been called "The Age of Anxiety." It's not surprising either that contemporary culture prescribes ego-feeding as the simple cure-all for inner emptiness and self-doubt.

Egotism and Self-Hate

One of the most difficult distinctions we need to make is the difference between ego and our authentic selves. They are not the same. Ego-feeding is not self-fulfillment. (I am speaking now of ego in the common usage, which approaches more closely the concepts of vanity and narcissism than the Freudian definition.)

Ego-feeding is the inappropriate process of convincing others and ultimately ourselves that we are okay—that we have value ("Don't I look nice?" "Aren't I wonderful?"). But the values we are catering to are not our own. Selfishness and excessive self-concern come from an inner self-hatred—the opposite of self-love. Egotism is a plastic imitation of self-esteem; its satisfactions are fleeting and hollow.

It is the well-fed ego, not authenticity, that is the standard of our culture, both straight and gay. The compulsion to need to be admired and praised undermines the courage to be oneself; it reminds one of one's inherent worthlessness.

Wealth, power, striking looks—the common benchmarks of success are standards for impressing others, rarely those of self-fulfillment. It never fails to surprise us that many of the people who are greatly admired by the public spend vast amounts of money on "shrinks" to find out why they are so desperately unhappy.

The vain, the conceited, the selfish all attempt to cover, but ultimately expose, their own feelings of inadequacy. They are like the bully who searches for someone weaker to push around, always in fear that someone with real strength will come along and shove his face into the dirt.

It should come as no surprise to us that, according to psychologists, blatant self-hatred is strangely akin to egotism. "One who despises himself is nearest to a proud man," says the philosopher Spinoza. Like the naughty child who draws attention by breaking things and hurting others, adults of low self-esteem often simulate self-importance by flaunting their misbehavior to get others to notice. Gay people have historically fallen into this trap—exaggerating their "unacceptable" behavior, because they do not believe they are able to be "acceptable."

Commitment

Authenticity requires accepting and loving yourself as you are. Discovering and being the unique you, in all your potentialities, requires discarding the limitations of your previous programming. This is particularly true for gays, bridled with the foolishness of the greater culture that we might be inherently less than perfect.

Somewhere deep inside, you must find the strength to commit yourself to discovering who you are, being who you are and loving who you are. Discovering your authentic self means piecing together the array of commitments that will make your life work. These could be grouped under four categories: commitment to your own creativity, commitment to other people, commitment to ideals and causes and commitment to accomplishment.

Underlying all of these commitments is a commitment to ethical integrity. Without respect for the rights and feelings of others as well as their need to find authenticity, there is little foundation for your own. Other people create the only context that can give life meaning. Our ability to relate to others is the ultimate test of our ability to relate to ourselves.

Love

From the moment we are born, we are alone. From that point on, life is a struggle to reconnect. Love in its various forms is our attempt to identify other people and things in the external world as extensions of ourselves and thereby plug ourselves back into the universe.

As Erich Fromm explained so perfectly in his classic book, *The Art of Loving*,[3] love is an attempt to share that which we are with another person, but in order to have anything worth sharing we must first learn to love ourselves.

Love takes many forms, from lust to romantic love, friendship, love of family, communal love and even something we can call transcendant universal compassion.

While lust has the most immediate nature, it is as quickly over as the physical act itself unless reinforced by deeper levels of affection. Love is measured by its mutual affirmation of worth. When lust lacks that affirmation, it backfires and decreases the feelings of self-worth in both parties. It is this lack of respect, rather than any characteristic of the actual sexual activity, that can make casual sex cheap and degrading.

Sex is a bodily function, a wonderful and integral part of being human. It is like the function of processing food. If we are satisfied and at peace, it will be just a part of life. If we deprive ourselves, through starvation or sexual repression, our bodies will make us suffer for it. If we hate ourselves, we can get hung up on the ugliness of sex, as some people get hung up on the ugliness of their excrement. If we find no positive ways of expressing ourselves, we can become excessive with either sex or food, pigging out, living only for the next meal or the next trick. If we are creative about our lives, sex and food become art forms that give our lives excitement and dimension.

Because self-love is the essential source of all love, relationships between people of low self-esteem are ultimately frustrating. Without this self-love, what passes in the name of love is mutual dependence. It lasts as long as the parties involved need each other and often ends in bitterness.

Our greater society dictates that women should find suitable men to support them and that men should find acceptable women to cook and keep house. We are told it is essential to have a live-in sex partner and produce children who will love (depend on?) us, and, in turn, take care of us in our old age.

Marriage is touted as some sort of magical solution to our problems. Ann Landers, the popular seer of our age, has divulged in her column the miserable truth—out of every twenty marriages, one is wonderful, four are good, ten are tolerable and five are sheer hell.[4] Gay illusions of finding eternal bliss "if only I could find the right lover" are probably as equally ill-fated.

Real love is based on relationships where individuals appreciate and affirm each other's potentialities. "I love you because you help me become the person I wish to be." All levels of interpersonal love develop from that main concept. Contrasting gender is hardly an important factor.

We may never know if the idea of long-standing, one-to-one relationships is instinctive to human beings or a result of cultural training. Romantic love is a cultural ideal that only a limited number of people appear to have the personality to generate. As Fromm points out, so many people wait for an appropriate love partner as a source of their self-esteem, not realizing that the self-esteem is the prior ingredient.

While the prototype of the long-term couple has worked for many, especially through the process of raising children, it is not fair to assume that all people, mature or otherwise, need an exclusive relationship to complete their lives. For many, the supportive ties of friendship and family or participation in a supportive community may be all the relationship necessary.

Community may be a gang of friends one hangs out with or a larger segment of the population drawn together by location, lifestyle, religion, common cause or profession. However, to be a valid manifestation of communal love, community needs to be a gathering that reinforces the self-worth of the participants.

Lesbians and gay men freed from the tyrannies of convention have developed fascinating new forms of relationship. These can be as successful as the standard in piecing together "human happiness."

Happiness

Everyone talks about happiness, but few are going there. Most people have no idea what it might be. They speak of it in terms of what it is not: it is not hardship, it is not illness, it is not loneliness. The therapists of those with wealth, power and fame will assure you that these things aren't happiness either, though certainly money can make one's misery easier to bear.

For most people, happiness means comfort, a release from the pressures of survival, fulfilling personal relationships, good health and some level of accomplishment in the eyes of the world. Other people imagine happiness as some state of natural bliss, akin to a drug-induced stupor.

Actual perpetual happiness is a state that exists only in dreams and memories. Life as we live it is always full of ups and downs, challenges, problems and disappointments. It is really only the joy we find in this moment that really matters.

"Joy is the affect which comes when we use our powers," says psychologist Rollo May. "Joy rather than happiness is the goal of life, for joy is the emotion which accompanies our fulfilling our nature as human beings."[5]

Psychologist Abraham Maslow spent most of his career studying people who were enjoying life, accomplishing and creating—fulfilling their nature as human beings. These were people who had achieved what he called *self-actualization*. He found several hundred of them and was able to draw a composite picture.

Characteristics he found included a sense of humor, a lack of fanaticism, tolerance of others, the ability to see reality clearly and a democratic spirit. Also on his list were acceptance of the unknown, calmness, the full utilization of capacities and success in interpersonal relationships.

The picture that Maslow drew was not one of people of great vanity, power or wealth, but of people who had striven for and found authenticity as unique human beings. These were people who knew the meaning of enjoying every moment. They displayed "the wonderful capacity to appreciate again and again, freshly and naively the basic goods of life, with awe, pleasure, wonder, and even ecstasy, however stale these experiences may have become to others. Thus, for such a person any sunset may be as beautiful as the first, any flower may be a breath-taking loveliness, even after he has seen a million flowers."[6]

Unfortunately, Maslow died in 1970, never actually presenting a path for us to achieve self-actualization. There are any number of people and groups only too anxious to show you *the* path to happiness, by which they mean *their* path. The truth is that there are as many paths as there are individuals.

For her 1981 book *Pathfinders*, following her best-seller *Passages*, Gail Sheehy polled 60,000 persons from the general population to assemble a profile of people of "high well-being" and how they got there. Her "Hallmarks of Well-Being" correlate closely with the attributes of Maslow's Self-Actualizing person.[7]

In the next four chapters you will meet lesbians and gay men who have partaken in the broad selection of available gay and straight lifestyles, philosophies and spiritual paths. The men and women interviewed have taken a version of the test used by Gail Sheehy (see Appendix) and clearly tested in the "high well-being" category. Their lives bear witness to the fact that a rewarding life is within the grasp of all people, gay or straight, with the courage to reach out for it.

In the final chapter of this book I will offer methods and approaches that you can use to discover your own path to authenticity and, hopefully, to well-being and happiness.

"Part of the difficulty in viewing homosexuality is that it is largely amorphous—a behavioral category of individuals who are about as diffusely allied with each other as the world's smokers or coffee drinkers, and who are defined more by social opinion than by any fundamental consistency among themselves. And since homosexuals differ at least as much from each other as they do from heterosexuals, it is not feasible to divide them into "types." Nor has an adequate understanding of their variations been gained by the attempts of various writers to describe "gay bars," particular groups, and scenes from the lives of a few individuals. The distortions implicit in any such approach are equal to those that would arise if one tried to glean basic knowledge of heterosexuality from visiting nightclubs, or from interviewing a few volunteers."

C.A. Tripp, M.D.
The Homosexual Matrix[1]

Chapter 2.
Lesbian/Gay Lifestyles

Those same faces, populating the same bars night after night . . . sometimes, a drag show—female impersonators lip-synching to the latest pop song . . . big dance palaces and small dance bars full of gyrating bodies, ripped out of their minds on drugs or alcohol, showing off their bodies and their latest boyfriend . . . perpetually horny stalkers, lurking in corners waiting for a promising look back before zeroing in on the kill . . . hairdressers and decorators with obviously bleached blond hair and overly-large pinky rings . . . young men in their 20s acting like a bunch of teenage girls, giggling the night away . . . average-looking Joes, fresh out of their average jobs, just out to mingle, run into a friend or meet the love of their lives. . .

This was the heart of gay male life forty and even twenty years ago, and for a good many men it still is. The AIDS epidemic has made major changes in this pattern, but it was changing even before that. Most of the men you will meet in this book might be found at a gay bar from time to time; some have spent many evenings drinking, dancing and cruising in this setting, but it's no longer the center of their lives.

Bars continue to be a meeting place for some lesbians. This is true especially in smaller towns where they may even share facilities with gay men. But in larger towns and cities gay men and women tend to stick to their own, and lesbians are more comfortable in healthier environments such as women's centers and rap groups.

If you try to understand lesbian culture by putting gay male culture to a mirror, all you will get is cross-eyed. Besides the ravages of oppression from the straight establishment and preference for sharing life and bed with members of the same sex, the cultures of gay men and women have as little or much in common with each other as they do with the establishment norm.

In a male-dominated culture, which would still gear women to being "just housewives" and "little helpmates," lesbians usually find their first responsibility is to establish their identity as independent women. It is estimated that as many as a third of all lesbians find themselves, or choose to be, mothers. Complicated by the greater difficulty in finding work offering reasonable support, this makes survival the key element in the lives of most lesbians and precludes the time for fashion and fancy exhibited by many gay men.

While some lesbians consider themselves separatists, who systematically screen all men out of their lives, the women I spoke with felt that such women were often fostering unnecessary hostility and missing an interesting part of life's diversity. They also felt, however, that during certain periods of their lives, isolation with other lesbians can offer women an experience of empowerment.

For the overwhelming number of lesbians, a long-term relationship with another woman and a settled home life are highest priorities. As one lesbian told me, "Show me a single lesbian and I'll show you a woman who just hasn't found the right lover." Only in the past few years has such pairing-off become a predominant pattern for gay men, as the threat of AIDS has made promiscuity and open relationships seem threatening.

Tom

Tom's childhood memories are happy ones. His was a "Leave It To Beaver" household in Southern California. Tom* was an adopted child whose parents spoiled and cherished him. While a bit of a mama's boy, Tom also adored his father, who would come home and roughhouse with him after work.

"I've always been extroverted and enthusiastic about life. I think I have a quality that makes people feel comfortable, happy."

Tom was popular in high school. He was on the football team and had a regular girlfriend. "The girl tried to push me into sexual situations, which just made me uncomfortable.

---

* All names in interviews are fictitious.

"I came out the summer after high school graduation with a fellow in his twenties who I met in the gym after swimming class. It felt good. I found the man extremely exciting. I felt no doubts and no danger. We took a long ride in his car each week after swimming class. My girlfriend was waiting for me at my house."

Tom worked his way through college, majoring in recreation. "I met the next man in my life at the hamburger joint where I worked after class. He was a man in his thirties. I remember asking him, 'Are there other people like us?' He brought me to bars and introduced me to gay life.

"From the beginning, I was attracted to older men. My father had been diagnosed with cancer when I was still in high school. As I watched my father get weaker, I was seeking men who were fatherly. My father died when I was two years into college and I finally came out to my mother.

"At 19, I met another older man, Mel, who became my first lover. I moved into his beautiful Hollywood apartment, and I was introduced to a world of friends who were older and well off. We entertained show business personalities like Rock Hudson. I was young and attractive and enjoyed a lot of attention."

After an extended period taking courses in junior colleges, Tom switched to a program in therapeutic recreation. He was already working in convalescent homes organizing community programs. "The old people really loved me and the centers liked me because I was generating all sorts of new programs.

"I had a difficult breakup with Mel. He wanted to keep me young but I was growing and evolving. I had only had sex with three men at this point and I was anxious to experience a more sexual lifestyle. Mel was the great love of my life and we're still friends today, but it was a father-son relationship and I couldn't grow.

"I was promiscuous and crazy for a while. Drugs were happening; the sexual explosion was happening. I lived in two worlds. I loved to dance and I spent a lot of time in the dance bars. This was Donna Summer time. But I also enjoyed the power aspects of the leather scene.

"I enjoyed older, stronger men, finding security in being overpowered. I was never into pain. I think I was working things out around my father.

"There were a lot of drugs, but I didn't have an alcohol or drug abuse problem. I was popular with a large group of friends who were all living the high life in the fast lane.

"I never lost my focus. I enjoyed being gay. I enjoyed meeting men, but I also enjoyed work and school.

"Just before completing my degree, I was offered a great job in business and traveled around the country as a salesperson. I was making good money in a gay industry. But I knew I was not really selling anything but my own personality.

"When I hit 30, I underwent a classic mid-life passage. I left Hollywood and the business scene. I had 'made it' in business with a good salary and it was time to move on.

"I enrolled in a college in a different city, changing my major to psychology, where I felt I could better work with people in need. I earned my undergraduate credits in one year and immediately entered the master's program.

"My present lover of two years was my rock and foundation through graduate school. I was too busy with job, school and volunteer work to even consider promiscuity.

"As I entered the master's program, AIDS had already entered my personal life. I had begun AIDS volunteer work. I had lost many close friends. I didn't want to limit myself, but that was where my heart was.

"For the last year and a half I've been an emotional support counselor in the AIDS ward of a major hospital. It's probably the most intense job you could have working with people with AIDS. In war terms you could say I'm 'on the battlefront' or 'in the trenches.'

"I've worked with a lot of people who have died. I don't get depressed but sometimes I feel overwhelmed. And I grieve deeply. These are my brothers. Their stories are often very similar to my own, so I identify with them. I'm 35, the average age of someone who dies of AIDS.

"To see so many people die at my age is to deal with issues of mortality, life values and spiritual growth. The things that come into play in work with death and dying are very maturing.

"I have gotten over my search for a father image. In my current relationship we are both independent adults. If anything, I am the strong one. AIDS helped me grow up. My life is full and rewarding. I have friends who appreciate what I do and are very supportive.

"I was brought up a fundamentalist Christian and as a child I enjoyed it. After my father died, I went to church Sundays with my mother. There were several sermons that were anti-homosexual. As I walked home with my mother after one such irritating homophobic sermon, I said, 'Mom, I can't go to church with you any more. It's just against who I am and it's hypocritical. I'm one of God's children too.' I gave up organized religion after that.

"I don't believe in a heaven or hell. But I do believe in a higher consciousness that I can contribute to. The way we touch the people in our lives is our immortality. The men that I have known who died of AIDS have touched my life and live on in me. The love I bring to this world will live on beyond my mortal body."

Tom appears to have tackled and successfully overcome a syndrome common in gay men, a particularly tacky mess that psychologist Jung referred to as *Puer Aeternus,* or eternal youth. This is a tendency to remain too long in the mindset of an adolescent—turning from job to job and from man to man—looking forever for the perfect gig and the perfect lover. The *Puer Aeternus* tries to remain eternally young, taking monumental risks and avoiding commitment, responsibility and routine.[2]

Our gay male culture feeds the fantasy and for many of us it remains the lingering barrier between where we are and any possibility of self-actualization.

The theory is that we wish to remain the-little-boy-that-mother-loves for whom no other woman will ever be perfect enough. Whether or not one buys into the theory, the situation remains—a great many gay men have trouble "growing up."

While it does encourage creativity, *Puer Aeternus* must be confronted and overcome before there is any chance of real well-being. Jung spoke of only one real cure—hard work with prolonged commitment.

Hard work can indeed have a cleansing effect on many ailments.

Beth

In her work clothes and blue jeans, Beth gets called "Sir" a lot. She owns a thriving construction business. Beth discovered her construction talents when she bought her first home and couldn't afford to have the work that she wanted done. Later she helped her friends fix up their houses as a hobby. "Even as a kid I always took my toys apart and put them back together."

Beth grew up with her father and stepmother in a home where she was physically and sexually abused. A tomboy with no friends and no real childhood, she left school to work full-time at 16. At 19, she left home for the Army and never looked back. She dated both men and women, but at 27 she left the Army, already two years into a 5-year relationship with another woman.

After a short stint with industry, Beth went to school to become a computer programmer. She found material success but little happiness.

"As a computer programmer, I was tied behind a desk eight hours a day and I did everything everybody else wanted me to do. I wasn't sure what I wanted. I woke up one morning and I thought, 'This is nuts. I have all the 3-piece suits and purses and $300 briefcases and I'm not happy. This project and those bills are due, so I can't call in sick. This is absolutely insane.' I figured if I'm going to live for about seventy-two years, why should I live sixty of those years by someone else's standards?

"I got up, went in and gave two weeks' notice. I sold my house; took all the profits and sunk it into the business. I sold my fancy car and bought a truck. That was two years ago. Now I'm broke half the time and I love it.

"I'm free because I don't have to worry about what others think of me or whether or not I have on the right suit for this business meeting. I don't like being confined. It's not that I don't like answering to people; I answer to people on a daily basis—the people I work for want commitments.

"But now I can take a vacation anytime I want; I can just schedule the work around it. Not that I've done that—I think I'm a workaholic. I enjoy the work for the sake of work. I can stand back and look at it.

As a computer programmer, there was no pride, what I did just affected someone else down the line.

"I've never been very feminine. I wore makeup when I was a computer programmer, but it didn't make me more feminine. It just affected my outward apearance. As a very dear friend told me, 'put me in a dress or skirt and I look like a dyke in drag.' I don't carry it off well. I have no problems with that. My clothing is all female clothing. It may be tailored, but it's female clothing, except, of course, my work clothes."

Beth's first love is now her roommate and close friend who helps her run the business. Beth's current lover is Suzanne, a nurse. "I guess there's some role playing," muses Beth. "I'm a lot more aggressive and masculine than Suzanne. She tries to be butch but she can't pull it off. Lipstick lesbians are more correct now, but I don't care about politically correct. But then I like to stay home and cook dinner; Suzanne would just as well go out and eat. I don't identify male, but then I don't necessarily identify female either. I'm sort of middle of the road."

Beth considers her lover and all her ex-lovers as family. Her community consists mostly of professional people, both straight and gay people she has met through her work. "They're people who like me the way I am." Also included are men and women from the gay church that she and Suzanne attend.

"But I didn't always like me. It didn't happen until I started making changes and stopped living for everyone else. I even started therapy this year to work out a number of problems I still have left, like my family. I am working at trying to understand what happened. I don't resent them. I don't think I'd change them—they didn't know any better and they made me the person I am. My therapist says I'm a survivor. I always knew that no matter how bad things got, there was a way out."

At 36, Beth sees her self-esteem coming from living her life the way she wants to live it and "treating people in a decent fashion, the way I want to be treated, not taking advantage of people just because I might be in a bad mood."

While Beth finds some strength in her Christianity, she has learned to look inside of herself for her gut feelings. "If I feel good from within, if I am happy with myself, with what I'm doing, it can't be wrong. If I love myself, then other people can love me, too, because there is something to love. If I hate myself, I do nothing but cause hate all around."

From Key West to Castro Street, from Christopher Street to Houston's Montrose, Halloween remains a gay national holiday and "drag," cross-gender dressing, is a significant part of that holiday. For most gay people today, that's where the game ends.

Until the 1960s, lesbians and gay men had few positive gay images, and many believed that by imitating the clothes and mannerisms of the opposite sex, they were somehow fulfilling their appropriate gay image. Confused gender identification blended into deliberate parody, with or without a sense of humor. The result was self-effacing; gays were caricaturing the basest in the other sex. Men imitated the shallow vanity, the clinging-vine passivity and the stark, flashy sensuousness of the most degraded women. Lesbians mugged the competitive, abusive, heavy-handed trappings of the grossest of macho men.

The past twenty years have seen these images dwindle. Drag queens tend to restrict themselves to certain bars, where they entertain themselves or put together shows to entertain the greater gay or straight community. In recent years, they have earned the respect of the greater gay community by fundraising to combat AIDS.

While drag may provide some exciting moments in the limelight, it is hard to prolong joy pretending to be something you are not. Alcohol and drug abuse run rampant in the drag scene and far too many men in mascara cry themselves to sleep in their beer after the show is over.

Gender-identified role-playing for both gay women and men within relationships has severely declined over the past twenty years. What remains is usually less a matter of "butch" and "femme" as one of dominant and passive. As with heterosexuals, individuals seek partners with personalities that complement their own.

Beth, as well as an increasing number of gay men and women today, as well as some enlightened straights, are uncovering in themselves possibilities of a different sort of cross-genderism—androgyny—uniting the best characteristics of both sexes. There are some women who have characteristics that are naturally and unabashedly masculine and some men who are gracefully and unaffectedly feminine. Why can't an individual be independent and assertive, as well as sensitive and nurturing? It may be that if they have the other aspects of their life together, such people may have an easier time reaching a high level of well-being than those stuck in conventional molds.

For other individuals, however, gender blending is not at all an issue.

Randy

At 30, Randy found himself powerless. Trying all his life to be a "good boy," he had suppressed his homosexual feelings. He was raised as a musical prodigy. His mother was a social activist who unwittingly made him feel guilty for not having activist leanings. He tried to do things by the book; he went to college to become a schoolteacher; he married a nice girl, a highly dependent type with whom he had a basically asexual marriage. He was miserable and frustrated.

While visiting New York City with his wife, they accidentally were spectators at a Gay Pride march. "It all came out in psychotherapy," explains Randy. "At first it manifested itself as depression—a feeling that I had gotten both my wife and myself into an inextricable mess. My first thought was suicide. One day I sat down with my wife and a close friend and said, 'I am a homosexual.'

"The situation wasn't good, but my wife's therapist made things worse. His attitude was to wish that homosexuals didn't exist!
"Finally, overwhelmed with the situation, I found my own therapist who dealt right-on with the problem and helped me with the process of coming out. He suggested that a trial separation should be incremental. I buried myself in Movement literature and helped educate my therapist. As I experimented sexually on the side, my marriage broke up—she couldn't deal with it. At a moment of crisis I moved out. It was difficult and exhilarating. I finished out the school year then moved to New York City.

"In New York at the tail end of the gay liberation movement, I wrote for the gay press. I was empassioned by my gay identification and I remain so today. I fell in love with another man in the arts and together we moved to San Francisco."

Today at 42, Randy is a leading gay composer and playwright. His plays deal with dramatically erotic themes.

Randy finds importance in his identification with the leather lifestyle. He enjoys the ambiance of strength and raw sexuality. He goes to the bars to unwind, listen to the music and sometimes to write.

Randy understands well the excitement of being able to give and take power, but is not into putting himself into serious risk. "My boyfriend is a consummate top; we have done some wonderful trips. It is like exploration of existence in connection with another person. It has given me an incredible sense of being loved and I am constantly uncovering insights about myself and how I relate to the world."

Randy lives with a roommate, but through his boyfriend he is involved in a complicated chain of interlocking lovers and lifemates. While he has total claim on nobody, he has instead a great deal of freedom and an extended family. He also has diverse friends, mostly from the gay community.

Randy is intoxicated with a high energy life that would probably shred the nerves of most people. His erotically-charged plays invariably receive mixed reviews when produced. He takes it all personally and then works out the anger through physical exercises and meditation.

"My self-esteem comes from my dedication to the gay community and to erotic liberation—a more basic issue. I don't believe in creeds. I'm a humanist, a renegade. What is important to me is figuring things out for myself; acting properly, ethically; offering good to the world."

While the super-masculine fantasy icon—the motorcycle driver, the cowboy, the construction worker—has always existed in the gay male imagination, cultural approval to role-play these images has only existed in the past twenty years. It is as if gay men have been given permission to act like men, and they love the idea.

Black leather is a symbol of raw masculine power. For a breed of men raised in fear that they were to be deprived of this power, leather is reassuring and fortifying.

Along with the leather images goes a form of sexuality that often is misleadingly called sadomasochism (S/M). While there may be some pain involved, as there is with most sexuality, it is mostly power games being acted out—intricate psychodramas, that may help the individuals involved work out deep-seated emotional needs.

In a growing number of cities, there is now a women's leather scene, a setting for acting out raw power—an exciting new idea for most women—and a vivid way of acting out their androgyny.

So much for the men and women dealing with power, but whatever happened to the sissies of our childhood? Some of them went macho, many live in the suburbs with a wife and three-and-a-half children. But some grew up holding steadfastly and proudly to their right to be different. Some have even become Radical Faeries. With a decided resemblance to the fairies that cavort in Shakespeare's *The Tempest* and *A Midsummer Night's Dream,* this rapidly growing gay cult can even boast over a thousand men connected by a computerized database. In 1987, West Coast faeries purchased an 80-acre ranch in Oregon referred to, of course, as a veritable fairyland.

Sky

Unlike most faeries, Sky's childhood started pretty much on the straight and narrow. He was an Eagle scout, on the honor role at school and vice-president of his junior high school class. His parents quickly forgot the summer he was arrested in the front seat of a car with an older man.

Sky was brought up as a Lutheran, which he accepted as a child, but remembers as being "non-joyous and judgmental." In high school he believed himself straight and had a steady girlfriend all the way through.

Sky hit college in the hippie days of the late '60s. He joined the theater club and, when he failed calculus, switched his major from science to theater. He took courses in dance and started to get in touch with his body.

After college, Sky got swept up in the back-to-the-earth movement and backpacked through British Columbia. He enrolled in graduate school in theater, while he and his friends squatted in a backwoods hippie commune.

It was in the free and easy hippie life that Sky began experimenting with his gay possibilities and found his first gay lover. Kicked out of graduate school for his radical ideas, Sky and his lover moved to a "hippie-faggot" commune where Sky supported himself through experimental theater. Finally at 30, bored with the country, Sky moved to San Francisco, where he still lives, close to the city's famous Haight-Ashbury district.

"In San Francisco, I finally learned the most important lesson of my life: *giving up, giving up*. Here I had nothing to fall back on, so there was no reward for giving up, so I persisted in crummy jobs and persevered until I succeeded."

Sky credits a lot of his self-discovery to what he refers to as "Son of EST" seminars that sprung up in the late '70s. "I came to see that I have a great deal to offer and that I had to learn to stop invalidating myself."

At 38, Sky has his own independent graphics design business, built on skills he learned in theater set design. He has an open lover relationship and a strong circle of friends mostly oriented to faeries in some way.

Besides the faeries, Sky is active in the general gay community providing graphics assistance to groups fighting AIDS and helping men find safe sexual alternatives. Before that, Sky found other causes to help him maintain his self-esteem.

What are faeries? Sky finds it difficult to offer a tight definition. "But there are certain beliefs a faery will likely hold: spiritual orientation toward the earth, which can manifest itself as earth- or pagan-worship; New Age beliefs; Eastern mystic ideas regarding oneness, with spiritual experience as personal and coming from inside; a delight in sexuality in a wide variety of ways."

Faeries also have a strong tendency toward androgyny, flagrantly giving vent to both their male and female sides. Camp drag is always in; faeries see no problem with wearing a skirt over blue jeans, or lace lingerie under a flannel shirt.

Aleatha

Born in a Northeastern city to parents from the British West Indies, Aleatha was taught pride and belief in herself from as long as she could remember, which is also how long she has been attracted to other women.

After high school, Aleatha left home to join the Army. She found lesbian life in the Army back in the 1950s active but closeted. When she met a lover, they both left the service, but the lover later met a man and married. Aleatha picked up the pieces and moved to New York City where she had a "grand ol' time" with her former Army buddies.

But Aleatha's life wasn't complete; she wanted children. She found an older gay man who liked the idea; they married and had a son. But her husband felt himself getting old and wanted his freedom back and they separated. Aleatha found herself struggling to survive as a single mother doing domestic work.

When she realized she wasn't succeeding, Aleatha resolved to remarry. She met a "nice man" who was raising three daughters. They married and had another daughter. Aleatha raised all five as her own.

"He was a wonderful husband," says Aleatha. "These ten years were a wonderful period. Unbeknownst to my husband, I had a 9-year relationship with another married woman during the day. We were both gay and married, and it worked. Fortunately my husband was more interested in sports than sex, so we didn't have much difficulty."

During this period, Aleatha went back to school and got an education degree and teaching credentials. "But the walls started closing in. I had a blackout and went to see a therapist. I realized I just wasn't happy, so one day I packed my things and took the youngest, who was 8, and my boy and I moved to California to live with my brother."

In California, Aleatha taught school, did daycare work and discovered the gay, black and women's movements.

Today, Aleatha is 49; her children are grown. She is still close with all five and has a "mess" of grandchildren whom she adores. She is a prime mover in the black gay community of her adopted city. She gives lectures on "Demystifying Lesbianism" and counsels women to help find themselves.

"Long ago, my mother told me, 'You are what you are, and do what you want to do.' I found strong values from my culture. God is important to me, but I see it personal in each individual. I was put on earth to serve humankind. I'm a good teacher and I care. I like to make other people feel good. I've been pretty happy most of my life, but I will admit that the happiest times were raising my children."

Racially and ethnically oppressed, gay people from minority backgrounds tend to approach gay life rather differently than middle-class whites. Being gay is the second cross they carry, not the first. This is reflected by the fact that most black, Hispanic and Asian bars are mixed men and women.

While the families of Hispanic and other macho-oriented, Catholic minorities tend to be highly homophobic, blacks are often more accepting. "You're our children," say black mothers, who often nurture large extended families. "Try to be discreet and we'll love you along with everybody else." Black gays often have trouble understanding white families, who disown or distance themselves from their gay children.

Aleatha believes that black women have an easier time dealing with being lesbians and a more difficult time relating to feminism because black women are used to struggling. Black society remains matriarchal and women commonly raise children without the regular presence of a man. They are therefore more likely to deal with their plight with resolve rather than anger.

Charles

Raised by his intellectual mother, a Bohemian modern dancer, in a college town in the Midwest, Charles always knew what it was like to be an outsider, but he also knew love and respect for his own individuality.

When his mother remarried, Charles took an immediate liking to his father's Quaker faith, which reinforced his individuality. Still, when Charles left for a top college in the East, he had few clues as to what he was to become.

Charles did well in school but did not find it fulfilling and he soon dropped out to work in a medical library and then a school for disturbed children. During this period he began experimenting with gay life and found it right for him. But he had not found what he was looking for as a career. Charles started seeing an analyst, whom he found helpful. Charles tried art school.

"But once again the energy disappeared. I tried moving to New York City. I found the city reflected the chaos I felt inside. I started taking dance classes for fun, which had been something I had done in college, too. I found teachers who were inspiring and found something in me. I took more and more dance classes, mostly modern dance.

"One day I sort of woke up to the fact that I was becoming a dancer. I realized that this was the only thing I had ever *chosen* to do and continued to do on an ongoing basis and I was getting better. It finally evolved into a career."

Charles set up shop teaching creative movement classes in New York and eventually moved to the West Coast with his first lover (whom we met earlier as Randy). Now, after twenty-five years of struggling, Charles is the leader of a highly-respected dance company.

While the money Charles earns goes mostly to support the company (he and his present lover share a tiny studio apartment in an unfashionable corner of town), he has obviously found fulfillment on his own terms. Charles' collection of books covers an entire long wall; the titles and scope of topics is impressive—lots of art, psychology and social theory. When he speaks of his dance company, he glows.

"I feel that my dance makes an important contribution to society. The kinds of dances I do bring the audience to struggle with themselves and their ideas of relationships and what it means to find oneself . . . triggering questions inside people."

Charles has had several lovers and even, for a short time, a wife. "Each of the relationships seemed to be like the changes in my profession and the aspects of dance I engaged in at a particular time. They have been like a string of beads, each a vehicle toward the next step. I have never searched for a lifemate; in fact, I rather like living alone. But for someone who likes living alone, I've lived with other people a lot. I discovered that when I was most content living with myself, I was most likely to connect with another person because I was connecting from strength and completion."

Today, Charles lives with Arthur, his lover of four years. Arthur is deeply involved in radical politics and socialism. Their shared community consists of Arthur's straight and gay friends from politics and Charles' friends from dance. Charles maintains active involvement in his Quaker Meeting.

Both men are lively, enthusiastic and very serious about their work. Arthur would likely rally behind his lover's words: "I feel the world is hostile to gays. The world is hostile to anything terribly different. They are hostile to modern dance, too, as well as to socialism and a lot of things I feel strongly about. But I have the strength to live the way I need and want to live."

Socialism and dance are only two of myriad things that can become the major thread in the lives of gay men and women. Creative arts of all sorts, professions, academic scholarship, hobbies, causes and charities give life color and meaning.

In the visual and performing arts, in the sciences, in the fashion industry, on college campuses and in assorted other places, gay lifestyles exist that are often far beyond the knowledge of most other gay people. In fashionable cities, gay cafe society dances and sings along to the wee hours of the morning.

Each of these subcultures provides opportunities for individuals to find their own definition of success and fulfillment. They can also provide individuals with the arena to act out empty vanity, aggressively degrade themselves or vainly struggle to meet the standards of others.

In many cities, executives who may know each other from the board room or the men's club, the yacht club or the country club, meet after work for bridge, for dinner and for sex. Many belong to the *correct* church. Some have wives and children at home in the suburbs. Many come from the *very best* families. They have been meeting like this for decades. Some are happy with their lives. Many die at an early age from excessive alcohol.

Professional women, too, have their groups with *additional* agendas and so, too, do certain ladies' clubs and civic groups.

Bud

When Bud was growing up, his parents moved so often he never had a chance to develop friends. As a young person, he had enough sexual contacts to know that he could go either way, but he didn't let it bother him. His religious background was negligible. Bud was fascinated by academics and school was the focus of his life. Bud dated a number of women and at 25, while still in graduate school, met his wife Nancy. Both were in the same professional field; it was an all-American romance.

Bud starting writing papers in his chosen sub-field, one which he pioneered. He earned his Ph.D. and was elected to the founding board of his professional society. Through the years his professional stature has grown and it has given him great personal pride. Bud and Nancy live comfortably, but are far from rich. Nancy is Bud's best friend. He loves her in and out of bed. Back in graduate school, however, Bud discovered that Nancy did not satisfy all of his needs.

"I don't think it's the sex so much as the emotional relationship with a man," explains Bud. "It was a matter of being emotionally mature but still wanting the close friendship with other men that I never had as a child.

"You can't get emotionally close to men who grew up with a homosexual barrier. You can have acquaintances but never close friendships. Men get together and bullshit about their accomplishments, how their stock portfolios have gone up and how they have risen in the company. They don't talk about emotional things—that's what I was looking for.

"One day, Nancy accidentally came across a letter from another married man who I was relating to. But she's pretty secure; she loves me—she understood. So Nancy and I have an agreement; she said, 'I don't care if you have a boyfriend, but if I find you with another woman I'll scratch your eyes out.'"

Over the years, Bud has had several relationships with men. Most have met Nancy. Some she liked; some she didn't. Bud feels that he's been in love with a couple of these men, but it never endangered his primary relationship.

Bud doesn't spend a great deal of time in the gay culture. When he does, he plays the expected masculine role. "I'm not comfortable with flits and sissies—I don't really know why not. I don't see myself as macho, that pays too much attention to an image that doesn't exist. My father raised me that real masculinity was a sense of responsibility, taking care of the family, community service and the rest.

"If I hadn't married Nancy, I'd probably be exclusively gay, but I'd be out of the gay mainstream. I'd probably want one man for the rest of my life and withdraw into a closed world. The best analogy might be the summer in the frat house I spent with my roommate/lover. When I wasn't at work, we were back there refurbishing the place. Maybe we'd go out for a couple of beers."

Is Bud kidding himself? It could be, but it does seem likely that he's managing well in his double role. Bud realizes how lucky he is to have an understanding wife who offers him the latitude to seek authenticity. So many people caught between two worlds are riddled with confusion and guilt. At 41, Bud finds his life an adventure and he feels himself "constantly learning and growing."

The bridge from straight to gay or bisexual is not an easy one. Many people struggle for a lifetime, never able to make the transition. Untold millions of people live under the guise of being straight, denying their natural drives for fear of losing everything precious to them, causing innocent people to suffer or leading themselves to hell and damnation. Psychologists identify these repressed souls with the title *latent homosexual* and society suffers from their psychotic maladies—everything from rape to child-molesting and queer-bashing.

A significant number of lesbians and gay men, like Bud, live part of their lives identifying as straight, then change their mindsets, and perhaps their clothes, to enter into another lifestyle where they are gay and out. Some of these people are bisexual, some are not. Many seem quite content with the combination they have put together.

There are still other people for whom their homosexuality has never become an issue. Ruth Baetz, author of *Lesbian Crossroads* writes about her early years:

I had met my love in college, and we had lived together for five years. We considered ourselves married, although of course it was unofficial; we were both women. Never did I attach the label "lesbian" to either of us. I rarely thought of the term, and when I did I simply assumed that lesbians were women "out there" who were probably sick or deranged and at any rate were trying to be men. For myself, I was glad Maria and I were women. Although I realized I would have to give up certain social and psychological freedoms for our relationship, it was a price I was willing to pay for personal happiness.

We had a classic "closet" marriage; we were an island unto ourselves. We confided our love to only a few close friends and drew all our deep emotional support from each other. When we met our first lesbian friends two years after our marriage, I was relieved to find other women who loved each other, but I was puzzled. These women said they were lesbians, and yet they were as normal as we were.[3]

Authenticity for most gay men and lesbians requires courage, strength and creativity. The straight world remains "the real world" for the vast majority of us. While we needn't be limited by its dicta, we must come to grips with them. The straight world with its inherent homophobia is a ferocious and threatening beast to most gay people, and each of us has to learn for ourselves how to remove its teeth and claws and teach it to heel.

Monty

Monty was a very lucky kid and one night, so was his childhood buddy. When, some fifty years ago, Monty's dad, an on-duty policeman, found Monty's buddy having sex with a sailor behind a dancehall, Monty's father scared them off and went back to his son. He told Monty that if he, like his buddy, preferred other men, would he please bring his partners home and be intimate in his own room, rather than jeopardize his future and the family name by getting arrested behind some dancehall. Monty was only 12 at the time and did bring his friends home. While his parents were hardly thrilled, they loved him and honored his preference.

Monty's life wasn't easy; being gay before Stonewall meant fearing arrest and pursuing a double life. He had some fun years during World War II, when he worked with the office that handled movie stars that went to entertain the troops. Later he worked for a major financial institution. He knew he never made the promotions he might have made had he been part of the social network, instead of going back to his gay life. But Monty took tremendous strength from his Catholic upbringing and from a very personal relationship with God. He believed in enjoying life and working hard and always had the respect of his bosses and co-workers.

Today, Monty is 62. He has never had a regular lover, but he has four "sons." He has met them through various classified ads. Monty is their "Dad." They range in age from 19 to 40 and they come to him for sex, love and understanding. His attitude toward them is that of a proud and caring parent, not that of a dirty old man.

Monty is active with Dignity, an organization of gay Catholics, and a gay seniors group. His smile is warm and everlasting. He loves to travel and share his exploits. When Monty discovered I didn't need him as a daddy, he became a friend and calls me when his sons enter contests—a couple of them are real *hunks*. He just came back from several weeks in the Soviet Union and was brimming with stories.

While Monty's story is not what the external world would describe as a success, he loves life, joyously accepts his sexuality, manages comfortably on a small pension and lives at peace, secure in his strength and in his values.

If this is what it means to be old and gay, it could be a lot of fun. Of course, in most cases it is not. Growing old is merely the last phase of growing.

Recently, I took a cable car ride up San Francisco's Nob Hill. Waiting on line behind me were two seniors, bemoaning how dull retirement was. Once I got on the cable car, two other old people got on and hung onto the rail. They were smiling from ear to ear. When I picked up their contagious grins, I realized the significant point about growing old—one can live constantly waiting for something wonderful to happen or, like Monty, one can enjoy the wonderful things that are happening this second, whatever it is that is happening. Gay or straight, it doesn't make a bit of difference—the attitude you develop in the bulk of your years will be the attitude you bring into old age

Carl

Carl presents a more typical example of a well-adjusted gay person enjoying his senior years. Carl grew up in a not-very-happy working-class family. His parents were Methodists, but he rejected it completely.

"My mother wanted everything conventional. She had me study music. I had early gay experiences but didn't think much of them. I joined an orchestra and since I was playing all the dances, dating wasn't necessary.

"When I was 18, I went away to the Navy and quickly learned the gay side of my nature. This was the Second World War. I enlisted for six years to attend the Navy School of Music. In Washington, D.C., I discovered the gay subculture.

"In the beginning I was 'trade.' I didn't mind what they did to me, but I didn't consider myself gay either. On my first ship I met a married man. We played entertainment for the crew. I immediately discovered I had no bad feelings about my sexual feelings and realized that this was my sexual direction."

After the war, Carl was stationed stateside and caught the eye of an Army officer passing on the street. They were lovers for twenty-five years. His lover was fifteen years older than he, and Carl retired from the service with him. Carl went to college and earned his bachelor's and master's degrees, teaching grade school for the rest of his working years. In the evening he played in orchestras.

"In those days, we mixed with both straight and gay friends. We went to the bars once in a while, but most of the time to each other's homes. We were mostly gay couples, living apparently as straight. I maintained a good relationship with my family."

In 1971, Carl's lover died and his best friend, a woman, died shortly after. Carl went to pieces, but maintained the continuity of his life through his teaching. He had a short relationship of one year, and then in 1975 he met his present lover of eleven years, also a teacher.

At 61, Carl and his lover are both retired and travel about half the year. Several years ago, Carl was diagnosed with Karposi's Sarcoma, an AIDS-related condition.

Carl's lover had a mild stroke at about the same time and they decided to enjoy totally the time they had left. They moved from a comfortable house to a large motor home that could be loaded and packed in one day. Last year, when they came home from an extended trip to Mexico, the doctor changed his opinion on the Karposi's biopsy and decided that Carl did not have AIDS. While they were thrilled with the news, they were also thankful for the impetus that had gotten them out of the house and traveling.

Carl has joined his lover as a member of a Unitarian church, although he considers himself an agnostic humanist with no particular spiritual feelings. Since retirement, he has involved himself with the formation of a gay retirement home, a gay seniors organization and political affairs.

Carl's life has always been one of moderation and, except for the difficult period between lovers, he considers his adult life a particularly joyous one. He has found self-esteem in his teaching, his music, his relationships and his organizational work. Carl has a community of mostly other gay senior couples, many of whom have been together for years; occasionally they visit gay bars and restaurants.

With only minor changes, Carl's life could have easily passed for that of a happily-settled lesbian. Through the dark ages women, even more than men, learned that happiness meant blending in and not being noticed. Even in these more liberal times, most senior lesbians are timid about identifying themselves and live their lives privately with curtains drawn.

Most of the problems of growing old gay are the problems of growing old. Loneliness, poor health and insufficient financial resources are major hurdles for old people of any persuasion. Our culture's obsessive emphasis on youth doesn't help.

Gay men, as straight men, often feel their identity creeping away with their looks and sexual prowess and may turn into mental lechers, ogling young boys rather than young girls. It is a problem of being old and male, not a problem of being gay.

The years beyond retirement are well-titled "the harvest years," because it is here that people truly reap what they have sown. To the degree they have developed strength of character, purpose, loved ones and the ability to accept life as it comes, people grow old gracefully. To the degree they have not, they become bitter and ugly.

"Religion does not help me. The faith that others give what is unseen, I give to what one can touch, and look at. My Gods dwell in temples made with hands, and within the circle of actual experience made perfect and complete: too complete it may be, for like many or all of those who have placed their heaven in this earth, I have found in it not merely the beauty of Heaven, but the horror of Hell also."

Oscar Wilde
"De Profundis"

Chapter 3.
Secular Philosophies

Like the man who was delighted to discover he was writing *prose* all his life, when he thought he was just writing, most people are surprised to discover that they have been living under some philosophy or combination of philosophies when they thought they were just living.

Juan

Juan is a happy man. His standards are pragmatic. He has been consistently meeting those standards and he has not unnecessarily compromised his integrity in the process.

Juan was brought up in a professional family in pre-Castro Havana. He remembers a life of comfort, culture and servants. "My parents taught me the importance of treating others well, especially the servants. 'They are family, treat them with respect.'

"I was always a child that knew my own mind. I had my own likes and dislikes. At 7, I was already reading literature and typing.

"But the revolution was hard on the middle class. I saw my mother jailed three times without reason. At 12, my family put me on a plane bound for Miami. My mother followed within a few months."

But Florida was no easy ride. "In fact, it was sheer hell. I had to learn a new language, a new culture. Mother was a professional in Cuba, but in Miami she cleaned homes. From that point my life became very serious. I was delivering papers at four o'clock in the morning. We didn't know what we would eat from one day to another.

"By the time I was 15, I had convinced mother to get out of Miami and 'Little Havana.' I wanted to be a real American. We moved to

Hartford, Connecticut, where the local Catholic parish helped Mother get a job in a comfortable location. We had a nice home, clothes, schooling for me, love and support.

"But when I reached 16, Mother had a difficult time with menopause and couldn't work. I left school and started my first full-time job, selling in a department store. I realized I would have to work hard and learn. Within four months I was department manager."

Before he was 30, Juan had already proven himself as a store manager and was moving up the management ranks in a large chain.

At first, Juan dated men and women, finding both perfectly natural. But when he finally accepted that he was gay, he decided to stop dating women and enjoy his natural bent. He fell in love with a man while he was vacationing in Miami and brought the fellow up North to live. They tried to be discreet and it lasted about three years.

"At 21, I sat down with my mother one evening. 'Are you gay?' she asked. I said yes. 'Is it my fault?' I said no. 'Have you been to a psychiatrist?' she asked. 'I have no intention of going to one. I know what I am and have no problem dealing with it. It's a lifestyle I believe I was born to and I have no desire to change it.'

"'The basic question remains that I am your son. Now you accept me as I am with my good points and my bad points or else you don't have a son.' She said, 'You're my son.' With that settled, I went back to concentrating on my career which was always the important thing. I knew the career would give me the freedom to be myself."

At 23, Juan met a man who was to be his lover for ten years. Juan grew tired of department stores and switched to the travel business. In a short time he managed his own office and taught a course on travel. When they were no longer happy on the East Coast, Juan and his lover picked themselves up and moved across the country.

Within a few years after the move, Juan borrowed money from the bank and started his own travel agency, which has become highly successful. One casualty along the way was Juan's relationship. "We broke up because we lacked common goals. My life was a success and his life was going nowhere.

"My friends today are both straight and gay, but mostly gay and mostly professionals with values similar to my own. I have no trouble dealing with both the gay and straight worlds. I am an individual; I act naturally; I don't want to be labeled. You either like me or you don't.

"I take pride in my responsibility, in my integrity, in meeting my personal and career goals. Possessions are secondary to me, but financial stability is important along with peace of mind, a place in the world and respect from those who matter.

"I believe in God, but I am not worried about the views of the church. I've turned to God in times of trouble, but I get most of my strength from loving friends and family."

Pragmatism is a fancy word for "making it" or "what works." This is the prevalent philosophy of every age. Survival—shelter, food on the table, material success, satisfying the standards of those who set them—that's what it's all about. Pragmatism teamed with ability, energy and integrity comprise the most commonly accepted formulas for success, especially when the goals are reasonable and personal like Juan's.

Without personal authenticity and integrity, pragmatism becomes a ruthless trap that consumes the overwhelming number of people in our times and in all times. It is the grandest of delusions and it makes self-actualization impossible.

However, not even empty pragmatism gets the sneering judgment of hedonism. Could a version of that philosophy work, too?

Phil

Phil was one of nine children of a Pentecostal minister and his wife in the deep South. When his parents decided to divorce, his father was excommunicated from the church and became an atheist. Phil grew up always being the "good little boy." He had a girlfriend, attended church and spent most of his time pleasing other people. As a project, he befriended the church "bad boy" and found himself having a relationship that went beyond friendship.

Phil's father also had a Ph.D. in psychology and believed that homosexuality was just a nasty phase that Phil would outgrow. So Phil decided to be straight. He married a woman who was his best friend and they lived together for three years, but Phil knew something wasn't right. When he read a novel on gay life he realized what it was.

At that time, his wife suspected that she might be pregnant and Phil felt he had to be honest and deal with the issue.

Phil went to a psychologist who asked him what his problem was. "I'm a homosexual," he said. "That's a state of being, not a problem," she told him. "What's your problem?"

"I'm a homosexual married to a woman I love, but I feel the relationship is not an honest one."

She agreed he had a problem and by the second session Phil knew he would have to confront his wife with the situation and get a divorce. He knew that she also was a person of high integrity and would not want him to be dishonest with himself. She did not take it well and wanted him to go and have it "fixed."

Phil finished out the school year; he was a school teacher as well as deacon of the church. Phil packed his bags and set out for Los Angeles—as far from the Bible Belt as he could get—to a career as an actor and the life of a homosexual, hoping that he could find a man to love as much as he had loved his wife.

Good looks and a Pollyanna attitude were not enough for stardom and Phil soon found himself redirected to a comfortable government job that let him off early enough in the day that he could concentrate on what was more important—finding a rewarding relationship and a good time.

"We're brought up thinking we have to be ambitious and have to go out and make a lot of money. I remember a conversation I had with a lover who was a bank vice president. 'I don't understand,' he said. 'You're one of the happiest people I have ever met in my life and you have nothing. You have a few material possessions, but no drive to make money. All you seem to do is float around and have a good time.'

"I told him to think about what he was saying. 'You're a sweet wonderful man. You have more material possessions and you're making more money than I'll ever make and you're constantly trying to buy things to make yourself happy. You work a 12-hour day, while I finish my work and go dance and play. Why don't you accept it: There's no place to go and nothing to get.'"

The greatest joy of Phil's life is his square dancing. He lives it and sleeps it. He's the organizer of a men's dance group and on the demonstration team that does shows at special events and fundraisers. His community is the other dancers and he's everybody's "best friend." He constantly has himself a "high old time" and doesn't see any reason for alcohol or drugs.

Phil takes a metaphysical approach to life, which he will have a chance to explain better to us in the next chapter. His hedonism has personal religious underpinnings but he's traveled a long way from Bible Belt dogmatism.

"I was brought up to be directed, to follow a game plan. I knew what that plan was at 22. I was married; everyone approved of marriage. I was a successful teacher. I was a church deacon. I was a well-directed, goal-oriented person.

"Then I discovered I was gay, got divorced and moved to a city I didn't know anything about and did not like: I didn't have any direction.

"I had dreams where I'd wake up in a field and I was in a car and there was no road to drive on, no place to go. But I began to realize that it was an even field and I could go in any direction I wanted. I could change directions or I could just stop. Then I realized that I wasn't going anywhere at all because I hadn't chosen a direction.

"Then I thought, maybe I'll lead a life where I won't set up expectations, where I wouldn't determine how life *had to be* in order for me to be happy. Instead, I'd try to be as honest with myself as I could be and even try to find ways to be more honest. That's what real growth is to me—to become more aware of who you are and what you are and knowing that all of that is being part of everything and a part of God."

Phil has been able to bridle in a responsible manner the philosophy that moralists have long condemned. Whether you think of it as *sex, drugs and rock n' roll*, as *wine, women and song* or as *eat, drink and be merry (be Mary?)*, hedonism is the philosophy that pleasure is the main goal in life. Certainly almost everybody has had some experience of throwing aside their better judgment and concentrating attention on the noble pursuit of whoopee. Alas, most of us have to face ourselves in the morning. It's hard not to be envious of someone like Phil who pulls it off so gracefully.

Rita

Rita is a person who proudly marches behind the secular humanist banner. A tomboy who grew up in an upper-middle-class, professional home, she chafed at the limitation of stereotyped roles. From the age of 7 she knew she wanted to be a doctor. Rita loved competitive sports and when she discovered in college that two of her closest girlfriends were lovers, she understood the meaning of sex, love and romance and "went for it." She found out that being a lesbian actually answered a lot more questions for her than it posed.

By high school, Rita had already rejected her Roman Catholic faith. "While there have been things I like about the church, especially the wonderful things they are doing in Third World countries and the concept of people being responsible for their own actions, I have trouble with the institutional trappings. I can't deal with God in a capitalistic, paternalistic, materialistic way. My spirituality has shifted from a God 'out there' to how we can best help each other out down here."

At 30, Rita is a physician and medical director of a health center that specializes in working with lesbians. Rita believes in medicine that deals with the whole person, not just a disease or a set of symptoms.

"The essence of being a good doctor on a long-term basis is establishing an atmosphere where somebody feels they can come to you with a problem. One wants to be efficient, but sensitive enough to find out what the patient really needs."

Rita reflects the same maturity in her personal life. It took a great deal of searching before she found a woman she could relate to honestly and completely. "She's also a very engaged person. She has talents she capitalizes on and projects she's doing. This keeps the relationship going. Both being busy and involved provides more for us to give each other."

Rita feels a special commitment to the gay and lesbian community, to other dedicated healthcare professionals, to her soccer team and especially to her lover. "We're very, very close."

Humanism is the philosophy that the moral aim of life is to serve one's fellow human beings—to further the quality of life. One can look at social responsibility as the obvious manifestation of humanism. It can be inspired by personal, secular beliefs or by institutional, religious beliefs. It can be directed to major causes or it can be focused more tightly with the people one meets in the normal span of one's life.

Many of the people we have met thus far in this book—Tom, Aleatha, Randy and Monty, for instance—are motivated by the desire to serve others. While largely unrecognized by the general population, gay people have long been attracted to the "helping professions." Humanism and social responsibility have long presented a loving course to self-actualization.

"How can I call myself Catholic given all of these transgressions against the rules? I can call myself anything I choose and no priest, bishop or pope can tell me otherwise. Each person's life is a major gamble. People who choose not to believe in God are gambling that when they die there will be nothing. I gamble with my life that there will be. As a Catholic who is also gay I gamble that the church has totally misinterpreted the Will and Word of God. If I am wrong then, the Church tells me, I will pay the price. Yet, I cannot conceive of a God who would allow a person to live on this earth as an emotional cripple when that person need not make that choice. Likewise, when the Church publicly condemns me and leads campaigns to eliminate my civil rights, they too gamble. If they are wrong (which I am sure they are), they will encounter a God who will greet them with 'How in the hell could you do that to another human being?'"

Brian McNaught
"Gay and Catholic"
Positively Gay[1]

Chapter 4.
Spiritual Paths

At least since the beginning of recorded time, humankind has been seeking answers to the questions of life and coming up with spiritual answers. As long as there have been societies, people have shared their answers with others or enforced them. Such has been the history of religious institutions. The great paradox of organized religion has been the need that people have found to resort to hatred and violence to serve their gods of love and peace.

The introduction of psychology has encouraged scholars to step outside the emotional trappings and deal with religion respectfully, as a tool humans use to find wholeness, without getting into the battle of which religion is correct.

William James, an American psychologist at the turn of the century, broke religion down into its component factors, explaining how these components each served basic human needs.[2]

A couple of generations later, Swiss psychologist C.G. Jung[3] took a dive even deeper into the human psyche and explained how all humanity shares a *Collective Unconscious* and mythological symbols (Earth Mother, Heavenly Father, Cosmic Self, etc.) that reveal themselves time and time again as we seek universal answers beyond the realm of conscious knowledge. Jung believed that contemporary rational/scientific men and women had not eliminated myth, but merely redirected it to the dream state.

Jung's "super-mythology" shows how in every culture individuals go through similar patterns of coming to grips with the aspects of one's personal being to develop a path he calls *Individuation,* toward an ultimate goal of merging with the Cosmic Self. Individuation strongly corresponds to self-actualization and finding authenticity.

In this chapter we will explore religious paths available in this country that provide viable alternatives to gay men and women. Once again, we will meet gay men and lesbians who are using these religions as valuable components of their own personal paths to authenticity.

Christianity

For thousands of years, few people knew that there was more to Christianity than the Holy Scriptures and the voluminous materials produced by the multitude of churches derived from that basic work.

In the 1940s scrolls began to materialize that were dated as far back as the accepted gospels that tell a very different story of Christ. *The Nag Hammadi,* named after the town in Northern Egypt where they were unearthed, are often referred to as the *Gnostic Gospels.*[4] While affirming many of Christ's teachings in the accepted scripture, these gospels expose a rich and varied tradition that formed the first three hundred years after the death of Christ.

Many of these gospels refer to a Mother/Father God, to sexual equality, to reincarnation, to female apostles and a female priesthood. Some even make reference to the evil, power-hungry church of Rome. There are those who believe that these Gnostic Gospels hold more truly to the teachings of Christ than the accepted scriptures.

Many scholars today consider what we call the *Christian* church to actually be more of a *Paulist* church, following the teachings of Saint Paul, often in direct conflict with the teachings of Christ. Saint Paul, Saul of Tarsus, never knew Jesus. In fact, according to the Bible, he was a persecutor of the Christians who saw a vision of Christ while journeying in the desert and was called upon to spread the word.[5]

The successive books of the New Testament tell of Paul's tireless efforts to convert the heathens. To further his work, Paul placed negative judgments on many of the practices of the pagans he was trying to convert. These practices include sexual equality, a female priesthood and, of course, the practice of homosexuality.

Paul also taught those that would listen that Christ would be returning "in their lifetimes." How strange that generations have clung to the teachings of a man whose one testable teaching proved invalid.

After the death of Christ, Christianity spread throughout the Mediterranean region. It was only the orthodox churches, centered in Rome and Constantinople, that looked to a consistent patriarchal doctrine.

Between the first General Council of Christendom at Nicea in 325 A.D. and the last Council in Constantinople in 869 A.D., the orthodox clergy selected the books that justified their power. They have even been accused of altering those books to reduce inconsistencies and further strengthen their hold on power and "the truth."

Historians agree that to effectively wipe out dissent, the orthodox church staged massive and bloody massacres of those who taught heretical (read that as "divergent") religious doctrine. So successful were they that it took over sixteen hundred years before copies of the forbidden gospels were ever unearthed and made public.

It seems incredible to think of the violence and bloodshed perpetrated by the protectors of the faith, all in the name of gentle Jesus, who taught peace, forgiveness and the inappropriateness of judging others.

Despite these skeletons in the Christian closet, it would be blatant ignorance to suggest that there have not been gay men and lesbians who have been among the millions who have found rewarding spiritual lives in every possible denomination of Christianity. Individuals have always had the ability to ignore those aspects of a teaching that they find unfulfilling.

Christianity, in every form, offers rich opportunities for community, ritual and the teaching of solid ethical values. It is only when an individual finds oneself being judged and found wanting that the specific church or denomination becomes, without a doubt, the wrong place for that person to be.

Gay Christians who feel divided by their gay inclinations and traditional teachings usually do well to check out parallel possibilities. Roman Catholics often find the more open-minded Episcopal (or English Catholic) church easier to digest. Many Episcopal priests are upfront about their lifestyles and some Episcopal churches have large gay congregations. Eastern Orthodox Catholic churches vary greatly in this respect.

Protestants often find a wide range of divergent views not only between denominations, but even among individual churches. The

United Church of Christ is probably the most progressive of mainline Christianity. It has ordained openly gay ministers and accepted into its fold largely gay congregations. The Society of Friends (Quakers) and the Unity Christian Church are so marginally Christian that they will be discussed in length later in this chapter.

Since 1968, when Reverend Troy Perry founded the first Metropolitan Community Church (MCC), predominantly gay Christian churches and gay versions of traditional Christian churches have been popping up all over the country. There are now over two hundred Metropolitan Community Churches around the country and overseas, preaching gay acceptance and a sort of generic Protestantism with responsible outreach within the gay community.

Dignity, a gay Roman Catholic group, celebrates Mass and offers congregational services to many Catholics. Actions by the Vatican over recent years have been making open support more difficult.

The Episcopal Church has an easier time with Integrity, its gay offspring. But the mother churches will have little or nothing to do with Acceptance (Southern Baptist), Affirmation (Mormon), Emergence (Christian Science), and Presbyterians for Gay/Lesbian Concerns.

Gay men and lesbians seeking fulfillment in gay Christian groups find strength in the combination of a loving Christian community and the ability to stretch conservative doctrine to bless their lifestyle and allow personal interpretation. Certainly, if Christian churches have found biblical interpretations through the years to justify the practices of slavery, apartheid, nuclear armament, biological warfare and genocide, all in the name of Jesus, stretching the word to bless an individual's preference of gender to love hardly seems like such a big deal.

Maxine

Maxine grew up the oldest of six in a "good Catholic family." They lived far from town so she played mostly with her siblings and cousins. Maxine was a tomboy who loved sports. When she made a few friends at school she'd "love them to death," but never thought that unusual.

Spiritual Paths

Maxine attended Catholic schools through college, serious about her studies and her religion. "I dated guys, but always preferred doubling with my girlfriends. I was a good Catholic—sexually naive—so it made little difference.

"I came out sophomore year with my roommate. We had an argument. When we went to make up with a kiss and a hug, it became more than that. Our relationship lasted eight years. It shouldn't have, but we didn't know any other lesbians. We hung out with another gay couple, two men. We played the old foursome bit. My mother was always trying to decide which one she liked best. I immediately accepted the fact I was a lesbian.

"I never had a problem with my Catholicism. I felt in my heart that this could not be something terrible and God would be accepting of it. I had more trouble with gay friends who couldn't understand how I could keep practicing. I told them I put aside all the baloney of the religion and hold on to the essence. I never had the angry feelings that others experienced. Nobody was ever terrible to me.

"Fortunately, I had written off confession before that. I didn't think there was any sin big enough to go tell another human being. Confession was in my heart and that type of relationship with my God was very important.

"I had mixed feelings about the sacrament of marriage. My mother wasn't allowed to take communion because she had divorced and remarried. That's when I decided that structure was not the important thing here. The church idea on marriage and divorce was crazy. Why stay together when you no longer love each other?"

After some graduate school, Maxine found a job with a large bank, where she has remained for twelve years, moving up to an executive position. "My style is strong and aggressive, but not masculine. I enjoy work and have always been real happy where I was going. Most people at the bank don't know my lifestyle. I don't hide it, but I don't flaunt it either. I'm only out to other gay people."

Maxine was delighted when she found Dignity. With her warm, competent style it was easy to see how she was soon elected co-coordinator of her chapter. "When I first started to attend, I thought to myself, 'How wonderful it would be to find a nice lesbian Catholic!'" And that's exactly what happened. Maxine's lover is a former cloistered nun, who left the monastery for medical reasons, discovering her lesbianism later.

Maxine explains, "My feeling of God is not so much a man as a spirit in all of us. I don't see God as a mother or a father. There is something in each of us that is God. I feel good about life and about God, but I don't know what is beyond life. I try to be true to myself and others. I feel the only mandate we have here is to love one another and bring each other around—just to strive to do as much as you can.

"I'm a lesbian. I'd be untrue to myself if I tried to be anything else. I wish I had some magic to have everybody understand what we are all about and to help them realize that it's quite natural. I know my feelings are there and I know I must be true to them."

Most of Maxine's friends are the men and women at Dignity, including Monty, the fun-loving senior we met in Chapter Two.

"I've never lost my faith in God," relates Monty. "On many occasions I faced tragedy and had to lean on Him. I always knew that God was there to help me and it always came out right. But I don't believe in blind faith nor do I accept the dictums of the Catholic church. I believe in birth control. I believe that people are sexual—homosexual and heterosexual. I think the church makes mistakes. After all, the church is people; *we* are the church.

"I feel that God is within me, too. I feel very good about myself. I've always stayed with the church even when I investigated other churches.

"I've been a member of Dignity for ten years. I liked it from the first Mass I attended—very friendly. I enjoy the gay priest and feel better with a supportive community. I also love the way we gays make a production of things. One Fourth of July, they came out with sparklers from behind the altar and a big American flag. The whole choir was dressed like they were from 'Oklahoma.' It's exciting; I even have non-Catholic friends who attend."

Judaism

To fully appreciate Judaism, the oldest religion still commonly practiced in the Western world, one must go back to its roots to realize what some four thousand years of Judaism have accomplished.

All religious teachers have had to apply their teachings to the words and concepts already understood by the people of that time. Buddha preached to the Hindus; Christ preached to the Jews and the Romans, and so on and so on. The early Jews derived from Mid-Eastern nomadic tribes, often existing close to the survival level.

The Jews introduced a theory of ethics and social responsibility totally new to that era. This was a morality of divine source, connected with sacred practice. While Westerners take this for granted, it was a breakthrough for its time.

The hundreds of laws developed in the Old Testament and related writings produced the longest lasting ethical code in history. However, as could be expected, thousands of years of scientific and cultural development have rendered many of the details obsolete.

Depending upon who is counting, there are three to five Jewish denominations active in the United States. They are distinguished basically by how many rules they reinterpret in order to render the religion practicable in contemporary society. Many American Jews follow little or no practice at all. They feel somehow different from their Christian neighbors but know few of the reasons why.

Judaism is almost always family- and community-oriented, which can make it tricky for gay men and lesbians to fit in, unless they conform to a straight-appearing nuclear family set-up. But bachelors, unmarried women and widows have always had a place in the synagogue and since Jews are often sophisticated and liberal, they often gracefully make allowance for family members who are "a little strange."

As with Christian churches, the attitude toward gays in straight synagogues varies. It would be safe to say there are likely to be a good number of gay Jewish people worshipping comfortably in traditional synagogues.

Lesbians and feminists, in general, have often found traditional Judaism unacceptable because of teachings that limit women to a secondary status. However, most Jews admit that women have played a major role in keeping Jewish culture and tradition alive and functioning. Also Jewish women today are often likely to be educated and expected to work outside their home.

It has been a Western Jewish tradition to start a new synagogue or a new denomination when individuals find existing interpretations too heretical, too fanatical or too limiting for their needs. The founding of gay/lesbian synagogues is therefore not as unprecedented as one might think. At this time there are dozens of gay synagogues cropping up in cities with large gay and Jewish populations.

Judaism is legalistic, but legalisms are always subject to reinterpretation. The same book of the Bible (Leviticus) that prohibits male homosexuality also condemns adulterers to death, provides that fabric must not contain fibers from two different sources and designates the proper birds to sacrifice when people come down with various illnesses. Be assured that even in the most orthodox of synagogues, adulterers are discreetly put up with and the local bird population is totally safe. In Jewish law, lesbianism is politely ignored.

Jonathon

Jonathon identifies as a bisexual. Raised in an Orthodox Jewish family, he found himself attracted to both sexes at an early age, but learned that his attraction to women was acceptable and his attraction to other men was not. At 24, while still in college, he met his wife. Together they brought up their two children, with whom Jonathon is still close.

"About six months after we were married, my wife announced that she did not want a monogamous relationship; so we tried an open marriage. By chance, the first couple we tried to relate to happened to be bisexual. I had never realized the state was possible and suddenly I realized there were others besides myself. I confessed my feelings to my wife and she thought it was great."

However, Jonathon and his wife realized that the life of active bisexuals was not appropriate for a high school art teacher and his wife in a rather conservative city and the family moved to a more liberal locale, where Jonathon pursued a doctorate in sexology, becoming a leading spokesperson for the state of bisexuality and devoting his life to furthering the cause of sexual freedom.

Jonathon's marriage lasted fifteen years, breaking up several years ago for causes he feels unrelated to their bisexuality. He is now happily mated to another man whom he first met at an S/M party, but ran into again at synagogue—a synagogue that specifically caters to gay men, lesbians and bisexuals. They both remain active (in the synagogue and the S/M community).

"I am a Jew. I enjoy the community and the ideology of making the world a better place to live. I believe in the sharing. It gives me a place to question my life. I can be Jewish and bring what I want to it. On Friday night, I can go from synagogue to an S/M party (with both men and women) without feeling strange. I know that the ethical values of my life are rooted in my Jewish background."

The Social Responsibility Faiths

America has a strong tradition of liberal faiths, where individuals seek to look past differences to emphasize the worth of all people and responsibility to humankind. The Unitarian-Universalists, Society of Friends (Quakers) and Ethical Humanists are the best known of these faiths. Over the years, it has been these religions that have been the vanguard in the battle against slavery and capital punishment, and for peace, sexual equality, civil rights and abortion rights.

The Unitarian-Universalists are the largest of these groups and still maintain some of the vocabulary of traditional Christianity—they have churches and ministers. But Unitarians cover a wide range of theistic beliefs. Some believe in Christ as God, while many see him as a historic teacher and feel little need for a God concept at all.

The Quakers are technically a Protestant denomination, but Quakers are taught to look for spiritual guidance from "an inner light." Pacifism, simplicity, human rights and service to humankind are practiced with a relentless passion by many Quakers, even when in direct defiance of prevalent pragmatic values and governmental positions.

Ethical Culture (Ethical Humanism) is a non-theistic outgrowth of Judaism, stressing the primacy of ethics and encouraging social responsibility and individual choices in spiritual outlook.

All three of these groups have taken strong public positions on the rights of homosexuals and many lesbians and gay men have found welcome arms in their communities. While intellectual acceptance is one thing, the reaction that a particular gay person may get depends upon the individuals at a given location, their personal hang-ups and their past experiences with gays.

Anthony

Anthony grew up in a Roman Catholic family with a strong ethnic identity. He always felt different from others and alienated from the Church. "A priest in high school told me that homosexuality was a sin worthy of hell. That was disturbing, but somehow I knew I was right and everyone else was wrong.

"I gave up the Catholic church in college. I didn't leave in bitterness. I left slowly. I just kept dropping a word here and there because I didn't believe it, until I found myself saying nothing but prepositions and verbals that didn't mean anything.

"Then I thought I was an atheist, an ethical person without God. But I met a Unitarian woman who was brought up an atheist and she remains the most non-neurotic person I've ever met. So I tried a Unitarian church and found it boring—they just talked a lot—and I didn't go back.

"The next time, I found a Universalist church (the denominations merged soon after). There were plenty of atheists there. The minister sometimes talked about God which made the atheists mad, and sometimes he made me mad, but that was okay. We had the right to choose what we believed. I realized what the minister did for a living made more sense than anything I'd ever thought of doing before.

"While studying for the Unitarian ministry, I had my first adult gay experience and it was wonderful. I realized there was nothing wrong with being gay. There were not yet any openly gay ministers in the Unitarian Church at that time. There were two of us ordained at the same time. My lover of nine years, a dancer, performed at the ordination and then we embraced.

"It took a while to find a church. Some had doubts that a gay minister could serve them, but I always had a profound effect on the churches I interviewed with.

"My present church did not have any particular gay constituency and still doesn't. They were just good people who practiced what they preach. They took to me and I took to them and I love them very much."

Charles, the dancer we met in Chapter Two, has had a similar love affair with the Quaker faith. "I find Friends Meeting such a delight because it's a chance to sit in silence with the support of others, to allow all of the outer voices of convention and belief to dwindle away so I can listen to 'the wee small voice inside.' If the voice is leading me to do something odd, then I'm encouraged to test it against or with the group: that's a sort of safeguard against madness.

"I went to a Quaker college on purpose and took a course on religion. But the course was very intellectual compared to my Meeting experience which was intuitive, emotional, unconscious and immediate. But it all seemed to fit together.

"All the brilliant and successful decisions and intersection points I made in my life, the choices were made intuitively, spontaneously, sometimes desperately, but they were right. Trying to deliberate and make rational choices never would have brought me to where I am and where I'm glad to be."

In my own life, I spent fifteen years as an active member and an openly gay man in an Ethical Society. There is no way I could ever express my gratitude for the love and acceptance offered me by those wonderful people, nor could I ever find words to express how their love has fostered my self-esteem.

Eastern Religion

It is often generalized that Western religion is rational, pragmatic and outer-directed, while Eastern religion is intuitive, mystic and inner-directed. Despite many exceptions, this statement holds a great deal of truth.

Over past years, Western psychology and religious thought have been growing increasingly closer to Eastern religious views. Our inner search for authenticity is based on such insights. Meanwhile, Asians are being infected by our pragmatic materialism. Note the rise of Chinese and Japanese commercialism.

An interesting note is that few religions, outside of those developed from Judaism, do not in some way incorporate the concept of reincarnation. While our scientists have no trouble accepting that matter and energy cannot be created or destroyed (although Einstein postulated that they could be exchanged: $e=mc^2$), the concept of a perpetuating spirit, which might also be beyond creation and destruction, requires more faith than most Western minds are willing to offer.

Buddhism

Buddhism is based on the teachings of Gotama Siddhartha, a historic figure of India in the sixth century B.C. Born a wealthy nobleman, Gotama explored various disciplines in order to find oneness with the universe. One day, after many years of searching, he came out of meditation while sitting under a Boddhi tree and achieved *enlightenment*. People sensed that he was different. "Are you a god?" they asked. "No," he said. "Are you a saint?" "No." "So then what are you?" they asked. "Awake," said the Buddha.

The Buddha taught that every living creature has within itself the nature of the universal (Buddha-nature) and that all human beings are born with a unique aspect of that nature. When individuals actualize their Buddha-nature in time it enables them to transcend from the suffering of this reality (samsara) to an unknown but infinitely better state (nirvana) which they imagine to be beyond, but is actually present and simultaneous; our so-called reality being far more subjective than we have any idea.

The various Buddhist sects have some philosophical differences, but differ principally in the teachings of the most effective techniques to realize and actualize one's Buddha-nature. Among the most popular Buddhist practices in this country are Zen, Tibetan, Nichiren Shoshu and Vipassana.

Zen traces its development through ancient China where the Indian sage Bodhidarma carried the Buddhist message. Here it made an easy alliance with Taoism, already common in the area. Indian Buddhism was highly intellectual and called for students to drop out of society to become holy men. Taoism was closer to the Chinese mentality—practical, in touch with nature and stressing the spirituality of ordinariness. While Zen flourished in China, it reached its greatest height in Japan from where it was transported to America early in this century.

Zen practice centers around Zazen, a stylized form of meditation, used to tune in with one's Buddha-nature and the universal mind. Zen students are encouraged to keep in touch with the world, but by maintaining clarity of mind transcend subjective thinking to realize a state of natural compassion and intuitive wisdom. The wit of Zen masters is famous, as they use unorthodox techniques to show students the foolishness of believing that things are merely as they appear.

Zen teachings, as with most of Buddhism, make no distinction between gay and straight. Teachings suggest that one should not degrade oneself or others through sexual exploitation and it is suggested that in time, with one's spiritual evolution, passions and desires become less important.

Zen teaches that the most important thing is to be true to oneself. As a famous American Zen teacher is quoted as saying, "Anyone still in the closet is not a Zen student." In San Francisco and in Los Angeles there are even primarily gay Zen Centers, developed as outreach to the gay and lesbian community.

Tibetan or Tantric Buddhism is a close cousin to Zen, but different in style because of its Tibetan ancestry. A major difference is the addition of tantric yoga (discipline) which works to bring the student's natural energies in line with the process of enlightenment. Kundalini or sexual energy is one of these energies.

The bizarre and mysterious art and iconography of Tibetan Buddhism puts off some, but not all, Americans, but homosexuality does not seem to put off most Tibetans. With the Chinese takeover of Tibet, several prominent Tibetan priests (lamas) have emigrated to the United States, making this a major center of Tantric Buddhist study.

Another group of immigrants—Japanese war brides returning with their U.S. servicemen-husbands after the occupation and the Korean

War—brought with them a simplified form of Buddhism popular in Japan.

Nichiren Shoshu Buddhism is based on the teachings of the monk Nichiren. Nichiren taught that continuous repetition of the chant "Nam Myoho Renge Kyo" and working to get others to join in the practice will bring chanters whatever they wish. Needless to say, the simplicity raises the eyebrows of other Buddhists, whom the followers of Nichiren, in turn, condemn for making practice unnecessarily joyless and complicated.

To their favor, these contemporary followers of Nichiren welcome gay men and lesbians, even if what they are chanting for is a new Harley, a deco livingroom set or a hot new lover. As chanters discover that through faith, life becomes an affirming experience, they grow to realize their own worthiness and can approach the Buddha's teachings with a positive, open attitude.

Vipassana meditation derives from Theravadan Buddhism. This is an older Buddhist tradition, still prevalent in Southern Asia, especially Sri Lanka (Ceylon). The Theravadans practice forty meditation techniques purportedly taught by the Buddha.

A growing number of teachers are working in this country, developing Theravadan practice for effectiveness with Westerners. Most of these teachers stress Vipassana or insight meditation techniques.

Vipassana sitting groups are springing up across the country, including women's and gay groups. There is also a full schedule of retreats for students to learn from intensive periods of practice.

Rachel

Rachel was brought up in a suburban Jewish family outside of New York City. Her parents were not religious and Rachel's mother shared with her daughter a deeply-felt resentment for the patriarchal aspects of that religion.

"All my life I've been identified as a nonconformist, as was my mother. I've had different belief systems, different politics. I've had an energy unlike other people's. I was searching for something I intuitively knew existed, something not available in suburbia, on TV or in the mass culture. I yearned to touch things deeply, to explore other states of consciousness. I knew there was something I had to find.

"In high school, I was an aspiring beatnik. In college, I became a hippie. I dropped out after three years. I was doing every drug in the book. All I cared about was drugs and sex."

In 1969, the height of the hippie era, Rachel moved to San Francisco with her boyfriend and other buddies to share fully in the experience.

"I came out as a lesbian through my boyfriend. Halfway through our 5-year experience, he told me he was also sleeping with men. I was totally fascinated and lesbianism suddenly became an option. It was all framed in a context of *free love*. I practiced bisexuality for two and a half years but the sex with women wasn't working—they were all straight women, experimenting.

"Then I got together with another lesbian and that was it. We came out together. We were each other's first lesbian relationship. That was fifteen years ago and we're still close friends."

However, hippie life was not all sex, sunshine and flowers. "I lost control. I took too much acid and flipped out. I went into an altered state of consciousness for four days steady, then more *on* than *off* for a month. I had flashbacks for years.

"It was very negative, but I believe it was all positive in the long run. It was a real kick in the behind. It got my life together, though I wish I could have done it more gently. It was sheer paranoia. I looked at everything that scared me. This is one way I can frame my coming out. I looked around me and realized that *men* scared me and *the city* scared me and I wanted out."

Rachel and her boyfriend moved to rural Oregon to help start a gay commune. It was here that she met her first lesbian lover. "After a year we divided the property into women's and men's land. We put in roads and water systems. We built houses.

"I was very proud of my lesbian identification when I discovered it, very proud and very 'into it.' I think it goes back to my being brough up Jewish. I was used to being a minority and immediately built up lesbian clan and family. This was the early '70s when lesbian culture was just beginning to bloom and blossom. We were creating

Lesbos. We were young and naive. It was exhilarating.

"Then I moved to a women's retreat center, still in Oregon. That was even more exciting. I was very involved in collective living. In two years, we did about twenty retreats in feminist and lesbian consciousness raising. We wrote a book to chronicle our experiences and it made us a small amount of money.

"By this time, I had broken up with my lover. I became heavily single-identified. There wasn't really dating in the country. I would make connections with women passing through. I would have loved to have had another relationship, but I was too isolated."

Since early in her first relationship, Rachel had been experimenting with alternative spiritual paths. "My lover and I attended the first Women's Spirituality Country Festival. This was 1973 and at that conference I was initiated as a witch (Wiccan). I didn't stay very long; I got scared by the magic. I wasn't grounded enough at the time. I was too close to my acid freakouts.

"We were all non-traditional in those days. I began studying lots of spiritual paths and psychic tools. I took a correspondence course in tarot. I studied astrology. I did peyote rituals in the Native American tradition.

"I was reconditioning my mind, giving myself new perspectives with which to look at what life was really about, exploring the ground rules to the life-force. I was doing this for about six years before I discovered Vipassana.

"My first Vipassana retreat was one of the most difficult things I had ever done in my life. I pushed myself very hard, to the point of breaking.

"I came out of that retreat seeing clearly. Everything made sense. I understood the interconnectedness of things. Life wasn't just separate parts; it had a unifying force. It's impossible to explain in words—it was an intuitive experience.

"I was working on my second book, an anthology of lesbian eroticism, when I discovered Vipassana. I had moved to another women's collective.

"I was with my long-term lover for seven years. I call it my marriage. When she started a relationship with a man, I moved to the city to do what I loved: study and practice spirituality. I am now going for my master's degree.

"My program is in women's spirituality. I am going to be a transpersonal therapist. Helping other women get in touch with their spirituality is very important to me.

"I support myself now by cleaning houses. I'm living meagerly—a student's life, but I find it joyous because I'm doing what I really want to do. I love school. Sometimes I'm dragged out, like when the vacuum cleaner breaks down, but basically I find cleaning houses grounds me.

"My mother is fine with all this. She's comfortable with my lesbianism. In fact, I think she admires my courage to be independent.

"I feel that through lesbianism and Buddhism I have found the depth I was looking for in my childhood. I have uncovered some of the most deep—and profound—parts of myself.

"Originally, my lesbian sexual experiences were so powerful, they threw me off-center. I didn't know how to exist in the world with that much power. The Vipassana meditation is grounding. Among other benefits, it helps me deal psychologically with my emotions instead of acting them out.

"Vipassana plays a central role in my life. It enables me to stay present and aware in the moment. I do sitting meditation every day, but the posture is not as important as what the mind is doing.

"I have some strong arguments with the Theravadan philosophy. It's been most sexist, but it's the practice I'm involved in. I've chosen primarily women teachers.

"Buddhist philosophy is important, but I feel I can borrow from the Mahayana (Northern) tradition as well as from the Theravadan (Southern). Some people simply follow what they are told. Others, like myself, try to follow what the Buddha taught, which is never to accept without question what a teacher or writing tells you, but to believe only what you know from direct experience."

Krishna Consciousness

The International Society for Krishna Consciousness, popularly known as the Hare Krishnas, is a survivor from the hippie days of the late '60s and early '70s. Like Buddhism, this evolved out of what is now practiced as the Hindu faith in India. The Hare Krishnas ground their faith in their interpretation of the *Bhagavad-Gita,* one of the most respected of the Hindu scriptures.

Their form of worship was developed by Chaitanya, a sixteenth-century follower of the god Vishnu, as personified in his avatar Krishna (an avatar is a god living on earth in the form of a man). Chaitanya reportedly would dance and chant the familiar "Hare Krishna" chant until he fell unconscious.

Followers of this sect dress in orange robes and put spots of paint on their faces. The men shave their heads except for a single, small ponytail. Hare Krishnas usually isolate themselves from non-believers and attempt to dedicate everything in their lives to Krishna so that they can become one with him.

Gay men and lesbians are welcome in the Krishna Movement. However, as one gay follower explained to me, " . . . while we accept that people in all states of life and types of lifestyle can make spiritual advancement, one makes the most advancement when one undertakes some austerity on behalf of the Lord. In our movement we may take initiation from a spiritual master when we agree to abstain from meat-eating, illicit sex, intoxication and gambling. Illicit sex refers to sex for purposes other than procreation. . . . I don't think that the issue has ever been heterosexuality vs. homosexuality."

Yoga

Yoga translates to the English word "discipline." Over the years, hundreds of gurus (teachers) have come out of India teaching various meditation and yoga techniques. What we commonly think of as yoga (hatha yoga) is a standard body discipline that has been used by many, gay and otherwise, for both physical fitness and spiritual advancement.

Peter (Purusha) Larkin, a former Catholic seminarian and self-styled tantric yogist, spells out in his book *The Divine Androgyne*[6] concepts for a gay male spiritual cult based on the mind-expanding effects of esoteric sexual activities. While not able to start a movement, he has opened new avenues of thought. There is reason to believe that such gay esoteric sexual activities may well have been practiced in the monasteries of many faiths.

Paganism

If you think communism gets bad press in this country, it's nothing compared to the nasty rap given to witchcraft and paganism. Paganism is a blanket term used for the earliest spiritual systems, the simple nature religions of cultures we demeaningly term "primitive."

People living close to nature saw spirit in everything—in animals, in mountains and in the stars. By paying homage to the spirits in these things they felt oneness with the earth and the universe.

Followers of these nature religions rejoice in their sexuality—homosexuality and heterosexuality—and often included sex in their religious rites. For most, the idea of judging this as wrong never occurred to them until so-called civilized peoples taught them to be ashamed of their bodies and that lovemaking was evil unless it was to create children.

It was uptight Christians who recorded most of what we call history, and they damned everything inconsistent with what they believed. Witchcraft never had a Satan or devil. This was a malicious attack by Christians on the nature god Pan who also had horns, but was associated with merriment and love of life, things that were evil only to the puritanical Christians.

Native American religions, voodoo from the West Indies, the animism of the Orient, the Celtic Druids of Northern Europe were all judged repugnant by the Christians who believed they had the only "truth."

As individuals in our civilization return to their connectedness with nature, it is not surprising that pagans and witches, or Wiccans as they prefer to be called, should be on the rise again and that gay men and lesbians should be among the vanguard of this movement. The faeries we spoke of in Chapter Two are often involved with this paganism. It feels natural and right and it teaches them to love themselves.

Helena

Helena is a Wiccan priestess, born to an intellectual but poor family behind the Iron Curtain forty-six years ago.

"I was the daughter of a famous artist. I was surrounded by models, philosophers, painters, sculptors and a lot of gay people among them. Mom was a witch. My entire family on my mother's side were herbalists. When I say witch, I mean Wiccan, Dianic, which was the dominant tradition in Mid-Europe.

"We relate to Diana, the Holy Mother. We are concerned in seeing nature as God. We have many traditions. Ours we call the Women's Mysteries, but there are also Men's Mysteries. Both accept homosexuality and heterosexuality without any problem. Men relate to the god Pan as the life principal. I have more straight women than gay women who come to worship the Goddess. When the sexes are separate they can get out of role-playing and can stop 'strutting' for each other.

"Being the daughter of a famous sculptor and heavy psychic and medium, I was always treated pretty special. People think *I'm* hot stuff; I'm a pale shadow next to my mother.

"My mother swore when I was born that she'd throw me out the window if I was normal. Father was a wealthy Transylvanian, a politician and a governor's son. He shut down Mother's studio and she promptly divorced him.

"The man who raised me was a famous doctor and healer, a strong metaphysician from a shamanistic tradition; he practiced nothing but mind power. He was the seventh son of a seventh son.

"As a small child I was put into a nunnery, because in post-war Europe nuns were the only ones who had food to eat and my parents were afraid I'd get brain damage from malnutrition.

"Mother was never concerned about my becoming a Christian. I was 6 already. She said to eat as much as I could and whatever they teach me just say 'yes' but don't believe it.

"It was in the nunnery that I learned about lesbianism. I was never a Christian but I loved the nuns. They were all coupled and it was easy to pick up what was going on. I had relationships with my classmates, but nobody knew there was a name for it.

"The Hungarian revolution brought political upheaval. I had to leave because I picked up soldiers on the street for my doctor-father to operate on. At that time, something clicked in me that 'things could be changed' and I decided I wanted to travel and become a famous writer.

"I decided I was going to have good times and laugh a lot, so I asked Momma, 'Momma, how would you feel if I escaped?' She said that would be fine. So she forked over all her cash, blessed me and said, 'Don't worry, just leave under the full moon and it will light your way and you will be very lucky.' And that's exactly what happened.

"In a week and a half I was adopted by the wealthiest family in Innsbruck, Austria. I was 16. They decided to take in a refugee and they chose me. They were proper Christians and I kept my mouth shut about my pagan background, but that was fine. I could take the Blessed Virgin Mary, direct all the prayers to her and it was as good as witchcraft.

"Then I got a visa and an international scholarship and went off to study literature and history at the University of Chicago, but it bored me. I knew what my tastes were, but I didn't know what it meant to be a lesbian, so I married a man and we had two children, but I was bored and started studying the craft in the back yard. The kids loved the candles.

"At 30, I secured a good Hungarian maid through my mother to take care of my husband and the children, and I hitchhiked across the continent. It took only three rides to cross from New York to the West Coast.

"I was disturbed at the time and I read a lot of feminist literature and joined a feminist group. I worked with other straight women and saw that the lesbians were having all the fun. I came out with a lesbian I met in a rap group. A year and a half later I fell in love.

"I had no trouble coming out; after all my mother wanted me to be 'not normal.' When I told her, she said that it was wonderful for an artist; men pull women down a lot. According to my brother, when she found out I was a lesbian she stopped worrying about me because she knew I would be fine."

Helena still lives with her first lover, sixteen years later, although they are now lifemates and no longer lovers. "I have a new lover; most of them last some time. I love to have a relationship."

At first Helena was a gardener, then she opened a candleshop and started her first coven, while writing books about feminism and witchcraft. She was a pioneer in women's spirituality. "The other women were not all big on the idea, but it made me happy and complete and we kept up the spirits of women whose traditional church gave them little support." Helena also runs seminars and does tarot readings.

"There are priestesses everywhere. Some are Dianic, some are generic Wiccans, all sorts of pre-Christian nature religions. They are for blessing; they are for sex, for life and for joy, for ecstacy. I feel rapport with all Wiccans, but find the others a bit boring. My circles are very theatrical."

What about black magic?

"There is no black magic! What we have is stupid magic and real magic. Stupid magic is attacking the innocent. Anyone that has had one lesson or read one book would know that natural law is self-policing; anything you put on somebody who does not deserve it comes back to you tenfold. Voodoo and other traditions live by these same natural laws. And as for Satanism, it is silliness created out of Christianity and has nothing to do with witchcraft."

Native cultures often realized that homosexuals were different and special, making them witch doctors and shamans, expecting from them all sorts of supernatural powers. Arthur Evans' book *Witchcraft and the Gay Counterculture*[7] documents a very different history of gays, witchcraft and the shabby treatment they've gotten through traditional accounts of history.

Generic Spirituality

Perhaps it's reflective of their basic optimism that, despite the fear and judgment of the predominant Christian sects, certain creative individuals have been able to trace spiritualism back to its positive, hopeful sources and redefined the higher power of the universe in terms of love, compassion and the affirmation of human worth.

The predominant religious organizations in this category are Science of Mind (or Religious Science, not to be confused with Christian Science) and its first cousin the Unity Christian Church (not to be confused with either the Unitarian or Unification churches). Both tend to be highly supportive of gays. Independent groups, such as San Francisco's predominantly gay Radiant Light Ministry, are also finding enthusiastic followings.

These groups follow the Sunday go-to-meeting format of traditional Christian churches but with a joyful "God is us" message. This is an inner-directed path which might be called applied metaphysics and should not be confused with the very different outer-directed social responsibility stressed by the Unitarians.

Alcoholics Anonymous (AA), Narcotics Anonymous (NA) and other twelve-step programs work on a parallel concept. Here, people who have been self-destructive exchange mutual support to escape their obsessions and turn their lives over "to a higher power." Extremely careful wording on this spiritual issue has kept AA and NA from getting into a narrow, dogmatic posture. "Higher power" can be interpreted in either a personal or religious framework.

Oppression from a hostile society along with other co-factors have led a considerable number of lesbians and gay men into alcohol and drug abuse. Such programs have provided a haven for many of them and for a lucky few the necessary impetus to achieve a high level of well-being.

Felix

Felix always remembers feeling more at home with older people and creative people. He came out early and attended art school in New York City, where he fell in with a sophisticated, gay, artsy society characterized by heavy drinking. As the alcohol took control of his life, he became alienated from his family, his future and himself.

Felix transferred to a school in the Midwest only to discover that the alcoholism traveled with him, but he had lost his New York support group. His life fell apart, he dropped out of school and he returned to live with his parents.

In a few years, he tried college again, this time in art education. And this time he went in for therapy as well.

"The first therapist I was assigned to was a homophobe, but it bounced off. He screamed at me and called me a 'cocksucker.' Even I realized I was saner than this guy. Fortunately, it was at a clinic and the problem was picked up by the clinical director who was gay and gay-affirmative. I went into therapy with him."

The therapy seemed helpful. Felix gave up on a destructive relationship and met a man who has been his lover now for over thirty-five years. Felix began working at a psychiatric hospital, but he was still drinking—often after work to relieve tensions that arose from problems with the hospital staff.

"I was very much in love but I continued to drink. I started switching jobs, doing well at each of them, but realizing that I was not doing what I wanted and not being creative. I was getting into trouble with the drinking. The only thing I had going for me was my relationship."

Felix went back to therapy and his therapist steered him to AA.

"Then the changes began—the whole business of looking at myself squarely, honestly. Where was I going? What was I doing? What were my values? What relationships did I have in my life and what was meaningful about them? I immersed myself in AA."

Eventually, after three years of sobriety, Felix enrolled at Goddard College in a special program on alcoholism. He specialized in musical therapy. "First I needed to identify myself as a creative person, an artist and a musician."

Still his problems were not over yet. One near-slip sent Felix back to therapy. He was pulling it back together when a work associate introduced him to Buddhism.

"Buddhism led me to accept many things and become aware of areas of myself that I had been fighting. All of a sudden life made sense and I was finding peace of mind. It was a natural flow for me from the spiritual underpinnings of AA."

Felix has been working with his own combination of Nichiren Shoshu and Zen Buddhism. He began working as a therapist with gay clientele in private practice, integrating his Buddhist thinking into his

Spiritual Paths

work. Felix is currently finishing up his Ph.D. in transpersonal psychology, a contemporary sub-field that combines traditional theory with spiritual insights. He faithfully continues his AA meetings, his Buddhism, his sobriety, his relationship. He's very busy, but it all works.

Still another kind of generic spirituality has a way of springing full-blown in the lives of individuals outside an organizational context. We met Phil, the responsible hedonist in the last chapter. Phil has his own personal spiritual understanding.

"When I was about 18 or 19, I was scared. I had been brought up a Christian and I was having a relationship with another guy. So I sat down one night when I was walking around concerned and said, 'I'm not sure I believe in you, Jesus (what I call God), but I'll make a deal. I need to believe in something. I'll believe you're real if I begin caring and having a good time, and I won't set any restrictions that it has to be a certain way. But some time between now and a year from now, I've got to feel life is exciting, wonderful and worth living. If that happens, you must exist because I have not done it on my own.'

"Oddly enough, a year later things did get better and I realized that if I did my best and just went along, everything would be all right and that I could take care of anything, no matter what was looming. Ever since then, that was God.

"If someone tried to label me, they would probably call me a metaphysicalist. I believe that all life is merely going back to being one with God. Over the years, this has become easy and comfortable. What feels right to me is what I believe; it doesn't have to come out of any particular creed or sect. I never base my concept of God on judgments, but on love. I am what I am."

Mysticism

Throughout history there has always been a certain breed of men and women called mystics who have felt they have an intense personal interaction with the universal God force. Some have claimed communication with forces or entities not embodied on this planet. Some of these people claim psychic gifts—reading minds, seeing auras, foretelling the future or even moving objects with just the force of their minds.

Individuals within the context of accepted religion who claim these special powers are thought of as prophets, sages and saints. Those beyond a religious framework are commonly thought of as "nuts."

Each of the world's major religions has had its mystics. Christian mystics include St. Theresa of Avila, St. John of the Cross, Meister Eckhart and Teilhard de Chardin. Jewish mystics followed a book called the Kabbalah. The Sufi are the Moslem mystics. Buddhist practice is all about the way to achieve mystical reality.

It sometimes seems that gays have an inside track on mysticism. One of the most respected books in the field, *Cosmic Consciousness* by Richard M. Bucke,[8] traces the history and writings of known mystics through the years. Several of those it follows—Socrates, Walt Whitman and Edward Carpenter—are known to have been gay. Many of the others are thought to have been.

To this day, there are a number of lodges, societies and churches that are dedicated to fostering the "mystic realities." Unless strongly under the thumb of a dogmatic, judgmental hierarchy, the groups tend to have the following elements in common: 1) a belief in reincarnation; 2) a belief in the ascent of the human soul beyond the earthbound condition to that which is sometimes known as transcended saint, archangel or bodhisattva, toward oneness with the universal God force; 3) belief in the ability of some individuals to communicate with these entities; 4) belief that all people are incipient gods with the eventual future of such ascendence; 5) belief in psychic powers as a gift of those making progress in such ascendence; 6) belief that each individual is unique and must discover his or her path through awareness of the universal already within his or her being; and 7) belief that it is inappropriate for people to judge others in any area of life, including sexual preference.

Among the best known groups following these guidelines are the Theosophists, the Rosicrucians and Eckankar. Smaller groups also exist. Also worthy of mention are the Fourth Way Schools following the teachings of the Russian mystic Georges Gurdjieff. There is at least one Fourth Way School that is geared entirely toward gay people.[9]

While those following religious and secular mystic traditions offer rituals and disciplines to develop psychic and mystic gifts, some individuals come to such revelations on their own or through close work with another individual. Today there are sane, ethical and educated persons who make their gifts available to others for counseling and healing.

A far cry from the storefront Gypsy fortunetellers, these individuals earn degrees and certification to add the official blessings of the establishment to the use of what they feel are their special gifts. Some of the individuals are lesbians and gay men. Gloria is certainly an interesting case.

Gloria

Gloria grew up the fourth and only girl child of parents who were intellectuals and socialists. "It was hard growing up with three older brothers. They picked on me. I was even molested. I was a frightened little girl and was offered little protection by my parents.

"There were few opportunities for bright little girls during the Depression. I was very lonely. I had crushes on female teachers and camp counselors but I didn't know what it was to be gay. I did have a wonderful time at camp.

"At the end of the war, there was tremendous pressure to get married. I fell in love with an ex-Marine and got married on my 19th birthday. I genuinely fell in love with him, and stayed in love with him for thirteen years. We had three children and I was very happy. In those days I dieted to be thin and tried hard to be the perfect housewife. For the first time in my life I was doing what I was supposed to do. I felt accepted. This was the first time I felt I really belonged.

"I went to college for three years while my husband was in graduate school. When he got his Ph.D. we left town, which was all right with me. The second year I was married I had a crush on a speech teacher—a woman—and I thought this was very strange. I didn't know what a lesbian was. I thought this was something evil in myself and I tried to repress it. Most of my fantasies were with actresses and musicians, so it got me doing music and going to a lot of shows.

"While church had never been an important factor in my life, in the late '50s it was the only place to find childcare and I found myself involved in the Ecumenical Christian Movement—very intellectual. By this time my children were getting older and I knew my marriage was no longer everything I wanted.

"Just about then I began to have my first mystical experiences. I shared a few with my minister, who listened politely and nodded his head. But this Christian movement tried to convince us that Christianity was a personal event, so there was a place for mystical experience.

"In 1960, I became seriously ill and it changed my life. I developed a tumor on my thyroid. I developed hepatitis and a kidney infection. I was beginning to become aware that there was a very deep unhappiness, a deep anxiety. I didn't understand the cause but I knew it was there.

"My being sick for such a long time was hard on the family. It took me out of the role of housewife and I started searching for meaning in my life. I was in my early 30s, but having married at such a young age, I didn't really know myself any other way. A psychiatrist supported me in my search and I decided to go back to school. I sensed there was something wrong in my life and I intuitively knew that I had to make changes.

"When I returned to school it was the '60s and I got involved with the whole student thing that was going on. I became a Marxist and a feminist. I dropped the church when I studied its attitude toward women. I became an active bisexual. I went to a lot of political demonstrations and turned my energy outward.

"In 1968, I got a scholarship for graduate work at a school far from the family. This effectively ended my marriage.

"By the late '70s I had finished my Ph.D. in sociology, had taught college and done political organizing. I finally met another woman my own age who I could relate to and officially told everybody I was a lesbian. My children were happy for me. My former husband was shocked.

"My friend and I traveled the country doing Marxist-feminist organizing. We ultimately found ourselves on the West Coast where I developed thyroid tumors and again got very sick. Bad doctoring when I had health problems in graduate school led me to have doubts about the medical profession. This time I found a holistic healer, who started teaching me to explore my own consciousness about my health. Skeptical at first, I remember telling her 'I don't believe in all this—I'm a Marxist.'

"But that was the time that turned my life around. I discovered the power of the mind to create illness and to heal. I learned to go into my own fear—to go into my own darkness, to accept that within me I had the power.

"Within a year and a half, I healed my tumor and started the process of healing deeper wounds—discovering my childhood abuse. I destroyed the tumor through visualization. I envisioned the tumor in my mind and then visually conceptualized and deeply concentrated on that which would get rid of it. What I had visualized was simply a group of little dwarves hacking away at it.

"I started reading material that explained to me the power of the mind, such as the *Seth Material*.[10] I began meditating and getting in touch with parts of myself that had not been well developed. At first, I started with visualization—visualizing what I wanted. Then I studied clearing the mind, which is what I now practice.

"I got in touch with the mystical side of myself. I opened myself to whatever energy was there and I began to identify guides. Visions appeared in front of me.

"For instance, when I was working with my healer she asked me to describe what the pain was like. I told her I kept seeing this image and she didn't know what it was. But she had a picture book of mystical visions over the ages. I looked through it and saw exactly what it was. It was Isis' rattle—the rattle to ward off evil.[11] Shivers went down my spine.

"So I opened myself up to that energy and it wasn't long before Isis appeared in my mind during meditation. Since then, I have spent a whole lot of time communicating with Isis and other guides who have appeared.

"All of this has opened up in the last nine years. There was a time in the past when I might have passed this sort of thing off as hallucinations, but now I know better.

"I discovered I was an intuitive and had the ability to do psychic readings. I also read auras and help people work through their past lives. I've learned to do hypnotism and trance work.

"I tried to figure out what to do with this. I started out helping my friends, but I knew it was meant to be my work. Last year, I decided to get my certification in hypnotherapy and almost immediately I had a practice. But I have never stopped in my political efforts. To me this is important toward understanding how lives express themselves on this planet."

The *Seth Material* that Gloria refers to identifies books written by the late Jane Roberts of Elmira, N.Y., between the years 1966 and 1981. These works comprise the largest, most comprehensive works allegedly channeled in contemporary times.[10] Channeling is the concept of the transference of information from disembodied entities (those who have transcended beyond the reincarnation cycle) as teachings to our reality.

The telemovie of actress Shirley MacLaine's autobiography *Out on a Limb*[12] in 1987 brought channeling to the level of a fad, especially on the West Coast.

Once again, the uncanny thing about these channeled entities is that their teachings, while couched in different metaphors, are highly consistent with each other and with traditional teachings. Needless to say, a good many lesbians and gay men are involved with this practice.

It seems appropriate to conclude this chapter with mention of the concept of the New Age, which refers to the heightened interest in Eastern religion, paganism and all aspects of the metaphysical, mystic and psychic especially in the last half of this century.

For some, the period is seen as preparation for the Millenium, the Armageddon or Messianic period long predicted in both Testaments of the Bible as well as many mystic sources. Beyond the original Christian churches, New Age people often see the churches as the Antichrist parading as the Christ presence, but preaching hatred, bigotry and judgment (as was predicted in the New Testament).

Gay men and lesbians are deeply involved in the New Age movement. Some would like to remind us that the period is identified by astrologers as "The Age of Aquarius," and that, in Greek mythology, Aquarius was known as Ganymede, the water carrier of the gods—and the gay lover of Zeus.

God made a little Gentian.
It tried to be a rose
And failed; and all the Summer laughed.
But just before the Snows,

There rose a Purple Creature,
That ravished all the Hill,
And Summer hid her Forehead,
And Mockery was still.

The Frosts were her condition.
The Tyrian would not come
Until the North invoke it.
Creator, shall I bloom?

                Emily Dickinson

Chapter 5.
Developing Your Unique Self

While you may be full-grown, the seed of your uniqueness may still be dormant inside of you. Or it may be that persistent weed in your garden that manages to come back over and over again. You try to kill it; it's weird and strange. You've been taught it doesn't belong in a proper garden, but still it returns.

If one day you discover that seed or weed and you cultivate it, clearing away all the other flowers and accumulated garbage, you just might discover that this plant will provide for all of your needs and bring your life peace and harmony.

The people you have been meeting in this book have been cultivating their own uniqueness. For most, there was much agony before they finally resolved to be that which they are.

As long as you are alive, that which is your uniqueness is also alive. All of the pain you are going through, all of your past mistakes are fertilizer that will make your plant bloom stronger and brighter. The great sadness is dying, never having enjoyed the happiness of being yourself.

I remember a time when I was 13 years old, an unhappy, lonely little boy, a sissy and a nerd the other kids picked on. I sat in the back of Latin class and wrote a poem and I knew that it was good. It was at just about that time I discovered a poet in English class whose poems made sense to me and whose ideas echoed the thoughts deep inside of me. My parents bought me a book of her poems.

I was still a sissy and a nerd and the kids still picked on me—my path was not easy. But I can trace every great happiness in my life back to the time I discovered I could write and I had a person on whose ideas I could role-model my own. It was another ten years before I discovered that I was gay, and Emily Dickinson probably was as well.

This chapter will present you with ways to discover your uniqueness, how to cultivate it and how to love it.

Real happiness, self-actualization, is being yourself every waking moment. At first, this is difficult; you have a lot of garbage to process out. But once you've discovered yourself and felt the joy, it will seem perfectly natural and will be with you to guide you through all the necessary ups and downs of being alive.

The mythologist Joseph Campbell said it all on public televison and became a modern folk hero. "Bliss is now." said Campbell.

"If you follow your bliss you put yourself on a kind of track that has been there all the while, waiting for you, and the life you ought to be living is the one you are living. When you can see that, you begin to meet people who are in the field of your bliss, and they open the doors to you. I say, follow your bliss and don't be afraid, and doors will open where you didn't know they were going to be."[1]

Self-Exploration

Who are you? After you have recited name, family background, physical description and a list of past accomplishments, go to your room and take another look. Here in the most private of places, you express the diverse dimensions of the personality you are presently acting out. Perhaps wedged somewhere in the corner you will uncover the persistent weed of your uniqueness. But just as likely that seed is still hiding in your top drawer.

If your room is a mess, guess what? Probably so is your life. If your room is a collection of artifacts gathered to impress other people, then these are the people who are probably determining the person you are trying to be. If your room is meticulously clean and neat with every item rigidly aligned, you may be compulsive and obsessed with meeting other people's standards and disowning your own. If someone else has taken over the look and conditions of your room, chances are, others have also taken over living your life.

But somewhere in your room is one or a few things that are just a little strange—a sketch you drew, a collection of fishing lures, a book on Etruscan pottery—things that are special to you that your friends would not identify with and your family would probably not under-

Developing Your Unique Self

stand. Such items are clues to your uniqueness. Fitting together the clues, cleaning up the mess and redecorating the room to reflect your creative self is a valuable first step on your path to self-discovery.

Values Clarification

When you're ready to continue the search for yourself in a more methodical manner, a body of material called Values Clarification[2] has been evolved to help people sort out what they believe and value. The material was originally designed for use with children, and this may be its greatest strength. When played by adults it can be both revealing and fun.

It works best with a group of four to ten people, with one person directing the flow of action. You each individually write out your response to the question posed, trying to be honest with yourself. Then you take turns reading your answers. Together you discuss what your responses reveal about your values and beliefs. Depending upon the question and size of the group, discussion should last one to two hours.

Here are a few questions that you might try discussing in such a group. But actually the possibilities are limitless.

1. Name the four persons living or dead you most admire. What are the things you most admire in these people?
2. If you should die ten years from today, what information would you most like to have included in your obituary?
3. If you could have three wishes for the world (affecting everyone, including yourself) what would you wish for?
4. What things in your life do you most like to (wish to) do? What things do you (would you) least like to do?

Before you start the discussion, everyone must agree that no one will judge another person's values. It must be assumed that everybody has the right to believe what he or she wishes and should be able to discuss these beliefs freely in an environment of respect. For the sake of discussion, a value is defined as a belief that you act upon consistently.

As you recognize your own beliefs and values, write them down in a journal and analyze what the sources of these values might be and how they are affecting your current behavior. Over a period of time this will provide a profile you may not have expected.

Your responses will probably vary a great deal from the others in your group. But listen and take an active part in the discussion. You will learn as much about yourself from your reaction to other people's responses as you will from your own.

Values Assessment

As we collect information about our beliefs and values, we discover that they are as contradictory as they are plentiful. Our minds have been compared to a confused jumble of tapes we are constantly playing back. We have tapes from our parents saying things like "You aren't as smart as your brother." "You can't do anything right." "Sex is dirty." Sometimes the tapes are positive like "You can do anything you want," or "We love you."

We also have tapes from schoolmates and friends that might say, "You sure are ugly," "Queers should be shot," or "You'd make a real good friend." Tapes also come from teachers, clergy, television—everyone with whom we come into contact. Certain tapes are memories of our experiences all by ourselves. All these tapes generate our beliefs and values.

Because our tapes are so inconsistent, and we listen and act on different tapes at different times, we are constantly contradicting ourselves and setting ourselves up for guilt and self-hate. Some people get so frightened they are unable to act at all.

If you have the money, you can pay a psychoanalyst thousands of dollars to put you on a couch and help you sort through your tapes. However, even with professional help, it will ultimately be your efforts that enable you to discard the ones that are doing you in.

The correctness of a belief or value can only be judged by two criteria: what feelings and emotions it elicits in you and how it works with your other beliefs and core values.

When you identify a belief or value, close your eyes and try to play back as many tapes as you can that led to the value, noting your feelings about these tapes as they pass through your mind. If the feelings elicited are pleasant like pride and joy, it suggests a value you might want to keep. If the tape brings feelings such as pain, guilt and confusion, it probably indicates two or more tapes in conflict, and at least one of them needs to go.

Another approach is to study the negative emotions in your life and the destructive behavior into which these emotions lead you. These can, in turn, lead you to the underlying faulty values and tapes. Such negative emotions and behavior include anger, fear, hostility, jealousy, worry, self-rejection, guilt and a good many more. *Your Erroneous Zones* by Dr. Wayne Dyer[3] details these negative emotions and offers day-to-day ways to overcome such behavior.

Another book, *Focusing* by Eugene T. Gendlin,[4] offers a method for seeking out the gut-level emotional clues to serious problems that are disturbing you. The book is fascinating and consistent with Dyer's, but at a deeper level.

Dealing with your negative emotions and behavior begins with bringing them to consciousness. It means learning to observe what's going on in your own mind, then taking the time to uncover the tapes that led to these feelings and the resulting patterns of behavior in your life. As you begin to feel the behavior coming on, you recognize the symptoms and learn to nip it in the bud.

Try playing a game with yourself. Make the assumption that you're always supposed to feel good. If for any reason you're not feeling good, immediately put your mind into gear trying to pick up what you are feeling and what faulty belief has led you to that emotion or negative behavior.

Worry, for instance, is the faulty belief that by concentrating on the things that could possible go wrong, things will get better. Think back about all the people who taught you how to do this, probably beginning with your parents. If you stop your mind from inventing situations that could happen and just spend your energy in the present taking care of what you can take care of, the worries most likely will go away. This is not easy to do, but it can be done and it's very worth doing.

I remember not many years ago, finding myself jealous of my roommate who had "stolen away" a boyfriend. Weren't they awful. I was upset and felt severely wronged. But I decided to work on the situation. I sat quietly and meditated, playing back my old tapes. I remembered how I had always been jealous of my brother, who my father obviously always favored and who always walked off with the attractive girls.

So for the thousandth time I forgave my brother and my father. I also forgave my roommate and my former boyfriend, neither of whom meant me any harm. I accepted the fact that I was playing back tapes of my own unworthiness and insecurity, tapes I thought I'd long ago cleared, but obviously had not. I also accepted the fact that you cannot steal another person's affections. If my roommate was more this fellow's style, that was a matter of taste, not of my worthiness. If they were insensitive to my feelings that was their shortcoming; why should I allow it to upset me? The pain was replaced with the joy of discovery and clarity.

My hopes are that I have overcome jealousy. Maybe with a little luck I won't be jealous of my roommate again and if the feeling starts I will know how to stop it. I thank my roommate for the opportunity for the growth process and now actually feel good about the situation as it occurred.

Overcoming Judgment

Almost all our negative thinking can be traced back to one thing—judgment. There is a good reason why Jesus said, "Judge not that ye shall not be judged," and the Buddha taught "Overcome duality—do not discriminate."

We busy our lives acting like movie critics, deciding that this person is wonderful and beautiful and that person is nasty and ugly. We judge that vegetables are "yucky" and desserts are glorious, or the other way around. Then we go about pushing our views on others, limiting their thinking and our own.

We allow our lives to be judged by others, jumping through hoops to impress them, or at least be judged "acceptable." We sell our own authenticity down the tubes in the process.

The fact is that all people can be wonderful or nasty; beauty is in the eye of the beholder and taste is taste. Most actions can be either right or wrong depending on the situation and what we know of it.

All we can really be sure of is what seems appropriate for ourselves at a given time. This we know and feel. No other label is necessary besides, "Yes, I want this person, action or thing in my life at this time," or "No, I do not."

The best way to learn to discount other people's judgments is to stop making them ourselves. You might try this Zen method: Walk down the street looking at everything, but judging nothing. Instead, you try to enjoy everything, saying, "This is perfect—This is the way it is."

Likewise, when you do a job you formerly didn't enjoy, try to hold back making a judgment and instead say to yourself, "This is as it is—a job that needs to be done. Anything extra that I add is simply a judgment I make, for which I may later be sorry." Attempt to concentrate totally on what you are doing, enjoying the pride of doing the job as well as it can be done.

In a Zen monastery, senior priests often take care of jobs like clearing garbage and cleaning bathrooms. Since they best understand the foolishness of judging these jobs as unpleasant, they're the best ones to do them.

Such mental exercise take concentration and discipline, but it can teach you how to take control of your own mind—to observe your own thinking and clean up your mistakes.

This kind of discipline can give you the power to turn off those old tapes that say you're *too fat, too short* or *too ugly*, or whatever it is you use to belittle yourself. How often you see a person who is shorter, fatter or less attractive than you, but walks with such self-assurance and dignity that nobody seems to notice or care. These things don't matter, because the person doesn't let them matter.

The bottom line is that other people's judgments should not matter, nor your judgments of them. The only judgment that is vital and important is your judgment of yourself and that judgment is only correct when it determines that you are fine just the way you are, *which is a fact.* This is the meaning of the title of the book, *What You Think of Me is None of My Business.*⁵

Centering

Sorting through our beliefs and values takes on greater meaning as we recognize and develop a framework that holds them together. The framework is composed of central or core values on which other beliefs and values hinge. The process of pulling together these core values is called *centering* or finding your magnetic center.

You can easily recognize people who are centered; they carry themselves with assurance; they don't let little things get them down; they take the ups and downs of life in stride, learning from their losses and mistakes. The people you have been meeting in this book are examples of such centered people.

Some core values are common in all centered people; others are uniquely individual. Additional beliefs and values are ultimately accepted or rejected in terms of how well they flesh out the bones of the core values.

Here are some of the core values all persons must accept if they are to find peace of mind and a high level of well-being:

1. I am fine just the way I am, but I am willing to keep growing.
2. I am a person of worth. I love and respect myself and I am entitled to happiness.
3. Life is worth living.
4. I have the will and power to guide my own life.
5. I can and will forgive myself and others for whatever has happened in the past.
6. All people have value and deserve respect, though I may never know why.

If one is to live a gay life, one needs an additional core value:
7. It can be acceptable and rewarding to be gay.

Other core values grow out of your experience. They can be expected to change and develop as you age and grow. Lifestyles, secular philosophies and spiritual paths are each based on their own core values. If you look back to the profiles in this book, you will notice how individuals altered and selected values from various sources, to piece together value structures that worked for them. Note, however, that every set includes the seven above.

Willingness

One of the important concepts in the first value listed above is *willingness*—to be willing to grow. This is no small issue; in fact it is probably the biggest issue with which most of us have to contend. There is no need to justify what you are or what you have done in the past. It appears to be some aspect of human nature to stagnate, to avoid change, in order to prove that what we have been and done in the past is all right.

But yesterday is yesterday; whatever you did was based on the best input you had at the time. Living joyously means avoiding getting stuck—opening yourself up to new possibilities, new ways of looking at things.

Whatever has been painful in your life is an invitation for change. In the following sections we will go over some of the basic tools for change, but they all begin with the *willingness to change*.

Forgiveness

Among the last words of Jesus on the cross were: "Forgive them, Lord, for they know not what they do." Forgiving ourselves and others is an important step in proceeding on. What others have done is their responsibility, but the scars and the anger are *our* problem.

The most significant ones to forgive are our parents. In most cases these people did the best they could, considering their own limitations. It isn't often easy to forgive those limitations; to accept the fact that our parents are mere human beings, like ourselves; to change the anger to compassion. However, for own sakes, it needs to be done.

Often within our anger toward our parents we can find clues to our own authenticity.

It is an almost universal psychological premise that unless one forgives and accepts one's parents, one can never fully love oneself. They are a biological part of what we are. Of course, this does not mean we have to enjoy being with them. But we need to accept that they are fallible human beings, like ourselves, responding to their conditioning. Gay men and women of high well-being, in almost every case, have forgiven their parents for even the most horrendous mistakes.

Phil's father, a Pentecostal minister, was particularly merciless about Phil's being gay. "Our relationship today is politely nonexistent. For many years I told horror stories about my father, but I got tired of hating and blaming him. Everything turned out okay, so obviously it didn't have a whole lot to do with Dad. And to feel an animosity toward someone who brought me into the world and did his best is just a waste of energy.

"So I came to terms with Dad. I love him very much. We'll never be swell pals being around each other but I deal as best I can. We used to fight every time we talked. But now I say 'Okay, Dad, if that's how you feel, that's how you feel.'"

Meditation

One of the most valuable tools of self-discovery is basically listening to ourselves. We are trained from early childhood to always be busy—to be doing something. Usually we are doing one thing and our mind is off in a dozen places.

Our minds are tuned in to so many stations that our thinking resembles static on the radio—we can't relax even if we want to. Things appear to get done, but the toll we take on our heads is costly. The ability to enjoy and appreciate requires concentration.

So what's the secret?

Psychologists sometimes call them relaxation exercises; the human potential movement calls them processes; Eastern religionists call them meditations. Call them what you will. This is a highly useful method of periodically clearing out the noise of our lives to give us the ability to understand who we really are and enjoy what we are doing.

Life provides all sorts of natural meditations. Losing oneself deeply in symphonic music is meditation for some people. Jogging or running is successful for others. Totally losing oneself in the creation of a work of art is meditation for still others. Free-form dancing can be an exciting form of dynamic meditation. The important thing is to clear one's mind from rational thoughts and totally lose oneself in concentration.

One highly effective method of meditation is breath-counting. You can do it comfortably by sitting in a chair with your back erect and your hands on your knees. Simply breathe naturally and slowly, counting your breaths silently from one to ten. After ten go back to one and start over. If you find yourself thinking or losing count (and you will), just clear your mind and start over again.

Mantra meditation, such as the once-popular Transcendental Meditation, is much the same except instead of counting, you concentrate on a short set of words or sounds that you repeat silently over and over again. Once again, the idea is to keep your mind totally clear of all thoughts.

Of course, there is controversy about which mantra is the best to use. "All is one" or "God is one" may provide additional affirmation to your life, if it makes sense to you. Eastern thought stresses the use of the sound "aum" as having a healthy resonance with the body and providing a sense of well-being. The Tibetan lamas claim that the mantra "Om Pino Pino Soha" will help protect you from AIDS. Maybe you want to try that one.

Another method of meditation is to lie on your back comfortably and consecutively tighten and relax the segments of your body from your feet to your head (making a side trip to include your hands and arms). Then imagine your body filling up with sky as you inhale, and emptying out as you exhale. Better yet, put on some soft instrumental music and imagine yourself inhaling and exhaling the music. (I find Brahms' symphonies perfect for this purpose.) On your back the possibilities of falling to sleep are much greater. In fact, this can be a wonderful way to fall asleep.

However, sleep is not the same thing as meditation and does not produce the same benefits. Meditation produces a state of deep relaxation coupled with mental alertness. This is quite unlike the state brought on by either sleep or hypnosis and just happens to be the physiological opposite of the state brought on by anxiety or anger.[6]

Whatever method of meditation you choose, and there are a great many others, try to keep at it for a period of at least fifteen minutes once or twice a day. Thirty minutes is probably optimal. Try to find a quiet place where you will not be disturbed. It is best to keep to a regular schedule. Upon waking, before the evening meal and just before retiring at night are prime times.

You can get additional benefits by also meditating at times when you are agitated or upset, or at any time you are in a mood that doesn't please you, including just plain boredom. If you concentrate on the mood and block out the situation, sometimes the meditation can lead you to the mechanisms behind your negative emotions or behavior.

Which meditation technique to use depends upon what works for you. Try one for awhile and then another. You can even keep two methods going for different situations or purposes. Think of meditation as a sort of mini-vacation from the world, a special treat you owe yourself.

The effects of meditation are quite remarkable. Some are immediate and some develop over a period of time. You will probably find yourself calmer and more efficient and therefore better able to cope with life's problems. You may discover more energy and maybe even a more philosophical approach to reality.

In bar cruising days, I found I always made out better after a good session of meditation.

Affirmations

Some years ago, a Frenchman named Coué advocated a system of improving the quality of life by repeating a saying that translates into English as "Every day in every way I'm getting better and better." In the 1950s Norman Vincent Peale taught "The Power of Positive

Thinking."

Most religions include repetition of some affirmation or creed, clearly delineating basic beliefs. Many prayers are actually affirmations of faith. Catholics may remember with horror the endless catechisms of their childhood.

Whether we affect some power beyond ourselves with our words and thoughts, or whether we affect only ourselves makes little difference; affirmations or prayers, silent or aloud, really work. They are an effective way to take control, to affirm our powers and self-worth, to solidify our core values.

Science of Mind and Unity are in the forefront of creative positive affirmations. Whether or not you wish to get involved with such groups, you can use a book or magazine of their affirmations. Our pansexual brother, Walt Whitman, wrote scores of poems that include affirmations of life and our ability to love ourselves:

> I exist as I am, that is enough,
> If no other in the world is aware I sit content,
> And if each and all be aware I sit content.
>
> *Song of Myself*

> I inhale great draughts of space,
> The east and west are mine,
> And the north and south are mine.
> I am larger, better than I thought,
> I did not know I held such goodness.
>
> *Song of the Open Road*

> The soul is always beautiful,
> The universe is duly in order,
> Everything is in its place.
>
> *The Sleepers*

Whatever the source, when you find words that are meaningful to you, that represent values you wish to incorporate in your life, write them down, paste them on the wall, memorize them. Repeat them when you wake, before meals, before you go to sleep.

Meaningful ritual can make your life richer, more decorative. Be creative. Sometimes you can add symbolic action to words—try hugging yourself.

Keep your priorities in front of you, and you won't lose track of them.

Visualizations

Here is another technique, often used in conjunction with meditations and affirmations to open ourselves up for change. Visualizations are means for changing our thinking by replacing negative conditioning with positive. There are, once again, many of books on the subject.[7]

One method I have found useful goes back thousands of years. I will imagine myself in a cloud of white light. I imagine each part of my body full of love and light. When I'm totally full of love, I try to think of the people towards whom I hold negative feelings—someone who did me wrong, a friend I'm angry at, or even a public figure who is doing damage on the national or international scene. Then I imagine that person in a cloud of white light, just like myself. I imagine that person smiling and happy. Then I do the same with anyone else I think of in that vein. When I'm done with them, I do the same thing with the people I like best and to whom I wish good things. I finish by saying to myself, "And we are all one."

One discovers that when you wish people love, especially on a regular basis, that it's hard to keep hating them. This is an effective visualization for forgiveness.

Seeking Professional Help

While the insights you reach from the ideas suggested in this book and others may provide you with valuable components for getting your life together, there may well be areas of emotional difficulty where you would be well-advised to seek professional help.

Besides mental health professionals (psychologists, psychiatrists, psychoanalysts, family therapists, etc.), gay people have also found strength and direction from clergy, substance-abuse counselors and other professional advisors. Group therapy and rap groups are sometimes an excellent, low-cost choice and can help you learn from the experience of others.

You don't have to be mentally ill to benefit from therapy. In fact, the people who benefit the most are often those who have the most going for them and just need objective help in specific areas. Most of the men and women interviewed in this book went for therapy at certain times in their lives.

It is important that wherever you go, the person be competent. however, for gay people, equally important is that the counselor be gay-affirmative. "Lesbian/gay affirmation therapy" is based on the belief that to assume a homosexual identity is positive, normal and healthy. The therapist does not necessarily have to be gay. But unless the therapist has gotten over his or her own homophobia, the counseling can do more damage than good.

The horror stories of gay men and women who have gone to therapists who have tried to change their sexual identities or invalidate them as individuals could make you sick. Therapists may seem fine and competent to straight patients, but turn from Jekyll to Hyde with gay clients. It is essential that you explore thoroughly before choosing a therapist.

If you lack the ability to do research in advance or are assigned to a therapist through your medical plan or low-cost, no-cost agencies, and the therapist starts saying that being gay is evil, a disease or a delusion, get out quickly—this person will do you more damage than good.

Dr. Marny Hall, a lesbian and psychotherapist, has published a book called *The Lavender Couch: A Consumer's Guide to Psychotherapy for Lesbians and Gay Men*.[8] It will probably remain a classic for some years.

In the book, Dr. Hall suggests ways to discover competent, lesbian/gay-affirmative therapists. Recommendations from gay individuals, professionals and agencies are probably the best way. Therapists who are themselves gay are often a good bet, but in many places these will be hard to identify. Experienced, open-minded straights may be just as valuable.

Another common obstacle is therapists without sufficient experience working with gay people. Several times we have spoken to gays who have found themselves wasting their time and money giving the therapists an education.

There are many good reasons to go to a therapist. Charles and Tom have gone to Jungian analysts to help clarify life direction. Felix turned to a mental health clinic for his alcohol problem. Randy and Phil found therapists to help work out the transition from straight to gay. Rita has used therapists to help her work out problems with relationships. Beth is getting help trying to heal the scars of her childhood. These people all report positive results. Many gay people go into therapy to get over self-hate or to accept their sexual identities—these are prime reasons, and often interrelated.

Anne

Anne is a person who today has found high well-being, but offers a lot of the credit to therapists with whom she felt safe sharing her feelings.

Anne's father died of alcoholism when she was 4 and she was raised as much by her sisters as by her mother. As the youngest, she felt her mother tried to keep her dependent, and her sisters and brothers each tried to make her into something different.

Until she was in her late 20s, Anne believed she was evil. She was fat and a tomboy with lesbian tendencies. She felt little love at home and rejected religion at an early age.

"But I had adult goals since I was about 8 or 9. First, I wanted to start an orphanage, probably to fulfill the need of giving to kids the love I wasn't getting. The dream went from an orphanage to an all-girls school. In fact, I kept that goal until I was an adult and actually did start a school."

Anne studied education in college, on scholarship. She enjoyed college and was active in college life, especially liberal politics. After college, she slimmed down from 250 to 150 pounds. "I realized I could not face little kids being fat.

"What I found was a whole new identity, a whole new self. It was like being reborn. I had energy like I never had before. I went out dancing almost every night and enjoyed being very promiscuous. For three months it was wonderful, then I got involved in a sticky three-some with a husband and wife, and found myself just as depressed as ever."

It was at this point that Anne sought professional help. She found a non-homophobic, straight woman who helped her sort out her confusion.

"I met lesbians through volunteer work with a lesbian hotline. I decided that these were the neatest people I had met in a long time." Within a month she was totally "out."

Soon Anne discovered her first relationship with another woman. This she recounts as the happiest point in her life thus far. But when her lover left her for someone else, Anne went into another slump.

After the breakup, Anne redirected her energy to starting a progressive school. She was active in the political/feminist/lesbian community and joined with others who were primarily anarchists in seeding a progressive school. The school was so progressive that the parents seemed to care little about her obviously lesbian lifestyle.

But Anne burnt out on teaching. "There just wasn't enough immediate gratification. I could work 24 hours a day, 7 days a week and never see the results of my energy." Emotionally drained, Anne turned to the political realm of non-traditional work. She became a union carpenter.

When Anne hurt her back on the job and could no longer work she went on disability and started speaking in high schools about non-traditional work. This led to work with non-profit organizations, which continues to be part of her life. But finally, tired of being poor, Anne turned to a governmental career in a position she finds satisfying and politically safe.

At different turns in the road, Anne relied on therapists to keep her on track. "I now go mostly to gay women, but straight non-homophobic women have been fine when I couldn't afford my choice. But once I spent $55 an hour teaching a straight woman about lesbianism and felt the wrong person was being paid.

"One of the biggest shocks was when my Mom died. It ripped everything out from under me and brought me back through my life. It made me more aware of ties from my childhood and taught me to face death. While I uncovered a lot of hurt, I finally decided 'I am who I am because of my mother and I like who I am; so, despite the hurt, it's all right.' I'm very thankful she was there. I think the greatest sadness was that she was not able to actualize her life.

"I went through individual therapy after Mom died and joined a counseling group, mostly lesbians. I was in the group for most of a year, learning to let go of pain and permit myself to be happy. I met my current lover in that group. Both of us have had counseling and therapy—it makes it easier to communicate.

"I have learned to trust myself, to be myself and to know that I am a good person. I don't know where I'm going next, except that it will continue to be a path of growing and being. I like not knowing what's coming next, but being sure that it will be okay."

Finding Love and Community

As we discussed earlier in the book, all healthy love springs from love of oneself. As we learn to know ourselves, we may find that we need a totally different outlook toward sex, love and relationships—an outlook consistent with the person we are becoming.

Western civilization has passed on to us a very narrow and often hypocritical pattern of acceptable interaction between sex, love and relationships. As gay men and women, we have the right to declare ourselves free to expand beyond role-models stipulated by straight society.

For a significant number of gays, especially women, lover relationships strongly resemble the traditional marriage. Some gays, like Charles the dancer, perceive themselves in the current phase of multiple relationships that last as long as the two partners feel that it is working and fulfilling (usually several years). When the time comes, they are ready to tip their hats, kiss goodbye and continue as friends.

As Anne explains it, "I got over my fantasy of 'one love forever' with my first breakup. Now I believe a relationship should last as long as the relationship gives both people what they want."

Phil, our responsible hedonist, stormed into gay life "looking for a mate." He is currently "between lovers" but not particularly concerned about it. "I've learned after some mistakes that it's okay to *want* a lover, but no good to *need* a lover. You have to learn to love yourself first. There's a big difference between being alone and being lonely. I never again want to think I *need* someone to be happy."

For Helena, our wistful witch, as for a good number of other gay people, an early lover becomes a permanent lifemate. Infatuations and sexual interests come and go, some move in, some do not, but there is one sustaining relationship that continues.

Of course, this is hardly the limit of choices. There are successful threesomes and foursomes. As mentioned earlier, Randy, our playwright in black leather, is part of a creative but complicated interlocking relationship of lovers and lifemates. Monty, our jolly senior, is a "Daddy" with a loving brood of "sons." Other gays, men especially, have an extended friendship community, where sexual sharing is a facet of their friendship.

Many gay men and some women enjoy a "heartthrob of the week" or just a lust for the night or a couple of hours. While these approaches are less likely to support stability, there is no reason to presume they are beyond the plausible options of men and women of high well-being.

The really important factor of a relationship is how well it suits the needs of the people involved. Too often the inseparable Bobbsey Twins who do everything together, and may even dress alike, are in real trouble; they are impeding each other's growth.

A healthy relationship is based on independent people, enjoying each other but also growing and enjoying space and time alone. Healthy people are concerned about their loved ones growing to fulfill their own potentialities. Unhealthy relationships are based on individuals expected to live out each other's fantasies. Possessiveness is a clear sign of insecurity.

Psychologists tell us that self-sacrifice and martyrdom, either for a lover or anyone else, is fundamentally destructive. What we are actually expressing in such behavior is that the welfare of another person is more important than our own. This is nonsense.

We do nobody a favor when we make them dependent on us. Alcoholics Anonymous makes a good point on this subject. People who live their lives cleaning up after drunks are labeled co-alcoholics and held responsible for prolonging situations where alcoholics are not pressured by need to find the strength to help themselves.

Self-sacrifice is not to be confused with a positive commitment to others. Commitment is enriching; it increases self-esteem. You are concerned for both your self-respect and the self-respect of the other. It asks no thanks.

Self-sacrifice leaves you feeling used and incomplete. It undermines well-being. Many situations combine and interweave the two and require careful sorting and weighing, which can still leave one in a "Catch-22" situation. Handling such situations well requires both thought and creativity. Leaving a dependent lover is tough, but leaving family, especially children and dependent parents, is even more heart-wrenching.

Three of the women whom we have met in this book, made the decision to leave behind children in their quest for themselves. It was never an easy decision, but in each case, they do not regret it. In each case, their children still love them and respect their decision.

Friendship, family and community are as precious to gay people as to straights. One is foolish to undervalue the importance of support systems to help us celebrate the good times and aid us through the ups and downs of our lives. Often lovers are too close to us to offer help when we need it, and it is important to have someone to turn to when one-to-one relationships hit hard times or go on the rocks.

Besides our own blood, gay people learn to make family out of ex-spouses, ex-lovers, lovers' ex-lovers and even past and present roommates. Once we have given our love to a person, that love and a little bit of us is always with that person.

In times of growth, as we go about making the kinds of changes in our lives that this book suggests, we discover that changing our friends and sometimes our lovers is an essential part of the process. Like seek out like, and unhappy people enjoy sharing their misery and are quick to ridicule those trying to break out of the pattern.

As we work on developing ourselves into the kind of people we wish to become, it helps to spend time with others on the same trail. Most people of high well-being have friends in the same category. (Over a third of the people profiled in this book were referred by others in the book.) Part of this is a sort of natural selection, but often people on the grow are sharp enough to place themselves among people from whom they can learn and be inspired.

Maximizing Your Energy

Even scientists have trouble explaining exactly what energy means within the human body and just what forms it takes. We speak of physical energy, mental energy, psychic energy and food energy as if the definitions were clearly at hand.

What we do know is that a significant component of well-being is the ability to maximize the energies of our bodies to give us the power to follow through on what needs to be done. Proper nutrition and health maintenance, sufficient exercise and sleep, minimal chemical and physical strains on our systems—all of these are essential to physical well-being.

Power is the ability to concentrate and utilize energy. It is normally a developed characteristic, built upon repetition and discipline. Meditation and educational study are methods to develop and focus mental power, just as calisthenics and jogging help us develop physical power.

Negative emotions are a significant way of draining off mental and physical energy. Anger, guilt, anxiety and fear burn us out from the inside. Positive emotions tend to feed our energy.

Another way we waste energy is to expend it every which way without focus. It isn't really necessary to see every movie, try every fad and keep up with every soap opera, unless those particular items are somehow particular priorities in our value system. A major part of the American population spends untold hours in front of the TV set, picking up useless programming and wasting time and energy that could be used in line with personal fulfillment.

Energy, like time, is a limited quantity. How we protect it, utilize it and maximize it will, in significant measure, determine what is available for our most important endeavors.

Experimenting

As you read the previous chapters, you met individuals traveling through a wide variety of lifestyle identifications and spiritual paths. Perhaps you have noticed that people of high well-being experiment in many places and take what they need from various sources.

Wherever you live you can identify where people participating in some of these lifestyles and spiritual paths congregate. Go pay a visit. Approach with an open mind. Meet the people. Try not to judge from your previous experiences. Be friendly; be respectful; be yourself. Most every group is looking for new enthusiasts. Listen and consider becoming involved.

Involvement does not mean commitment (the chicken was involved in breakfast; the pig was committed). Take things slowly, weighing alternatives. If you want to check out the leather lifestyle, go to a bar a few times and meet the people. Ask what they get out of it. Hold off awhile before you run out to buy a Harley-Davidson and get rings in your nipples.

Besides the areas enumerated in this book, there are many places, both straight and gay that will welcome you. Hospitals need volunteers. Performing arts groups are often supportive of gays. Political groups are always hungry for workers. In cities, gay causes abound. The crisis of AIDS has opened up countless opportunities for gay men and lesbians to commit themselves to a cause of real relevance.

Education is a life-long process. Adult courses are available at many high schools and college courses are available in most towns. Learn something new that may open up a new possibility of commitment or a new avenue of interest.

Assertiveness training courses are available in many places as well as the classic Dale Carnegie course, which is also available by correspondence. These courses can give you increased self-confidence.

There are also opportunities for programs to expand your ideas about yourself. Out of the human potential movement come seminars and workshops like EST and Lifespring. Most have gays involved. These programs are composed of bits and pieces of teachings from disciplines such as those we have discussed. While they should not be seen as ends unto themselves, they can open your eyes and broaden your horizons. They do tend to be costly and, while they can get you started, you will still have to go through the painstaking job of finding your own personal path. Sky, the designer-faery, traced the change in his life to such seminars.

Gay men and lesbians have also been giving rave reviews to "A Course in Miracles."[9] This is a dramatic program of reading and exercises for spiritual uplift consistent with the kind of thinking in Science of Mind. The course is self-administered and costs about $40 for the necessary books. However, it would be well to leaf through the material before making the investment—it is not for everyone.

Moving On

You cannot run away from yourself, but you can escape persecution. Unless you choose to spend your life in the closet, to be yourself requires validation from a loving, accepting community. Gay people rarely find such validation alone in small-town America, the Bible Belt, or the deep South. If the words queer, dyke, sissy or faggot are echoing through your brain, then it's probably time to pack up and move out. You have several choices.

Almost all big cities have large gay communities, but big cities require survival skills that you may or may not have. Job training and experience is vital when you move to a big city; they are notorious for chewing up and spitting out kids who wander in young and unskilled. On the other hand, gay professionals, artists and craftspersons will find sophisticated cities full of opportunities and supportive communities.

Large cities will also give you the maximum opportunity to check out spiritual paths and lifestyles. Research the possible cities before you move—they are all very different.

Smaller cities and towns normally have smaller gay communities unless they have liberal college campuses or an established liberal tradition. Artistic communities often have large gay settlements, as do resort towns. But beware, glamorous spots with streets paved in gold usually have wide unglamorous gutters.

Rural America has more gay outposts than most people imagine. A surprising number of gay men and women sneak off to the wilderness to live inconspicuously in pairs or small groups.

Check the addresses on classified ads in gay publications to get a good idea of gay geography. There is even a publication called *RFD* that caters particularly to rural gay men.

If you move, leave with a positive plan and, if possible, a contact. The streets, Y's and bars are the worst places to get started. Immediately seek out places where you will be likely to meet people "who have their heads together," gay churches, organizations, professional groups. Make friends; let it be known that you are seeking to give of yourself, not to be taken care of. Don't let sex be your highest priority; self-respect must come first. Find work as soon as possible. Temporary agencies may be able to fill the gap until you find a permanent position.

There are lots of other good reasons besides gay persecution to move. Sometimes one moves for job opportunities or to distance oneself from family or an ex-lover with whom one is no longer able to deal. Sometimes you just have to get away and start fresh to establish yourself as the person you are becoming and remove yourself from a person, crowd or situation that is pulling you down.

But there are certain things you cannot run away from. You cannot run away from a low self-image. It will be wherever you are when you arrive. You cannot run away from a substance-abuse problem; it will catch up with you, one way or another, unless you attack the underlying cause.

But change is healthy. A new location will provide you with different challenges and teach you about abilities you never knew you had. All of the people we interviewed had lived in various places, and most in several different parts of the country. Staying still is a sure way of getting nowhere.

Getting Started

Just reading this or any other book will not help a person get his or her life together. The only thing that will put you on the path of high well-being will be to make the commitment and start the effort. Even intellectually knowing what's wrong is of little help—you must *effect change*.

When you finish this book, straighten your room, plan a trip to the library or bookstore to get the books you'll need to follow up. Begin to schedule visits to places where you can learn new insights into yourself. Put the book by your bed and keep reading over the sections that hold the most importance to you. Consider putting together a Values Clarification group. If necessary, find a good therapist.

Behavior modification is another winner. Start doing things a bit differently than you've done them before. Find a writing of self-affirmation that means something to you and tape it on the wall. Plan to read it out loud at the same time once a day. Give up a habit or, perhaps, a "friend" that is dragging you down.

The most important thing you must accept is that the point of power is *this very moment*. If you take control of each second, you take control of your life. Such control requires self-knowledge and self-affirmation. This will lead you to change, to some risks and occasionally to a few mistakes, but that's not bad.

The men and women profiled in this book were asked about the risks they had taken and mistakes they had made. Some of these risks were major: walking out on everything they had ever known, traveling across the country to an unknown destination. There were also monumental mistakes, including bad investments, trying to run away from themselves and destructive relationships.

But one thread ran through these tales of risks and mistakes—"It was worth it." Every mistake brought with it a bonanza of new information about themselves and the world. It was often the most devastating mistake that led to the important insights that made life ultimately work.

Taking risks in your life does not mean flying high on wild gambles or crazy escapades. We are talking about investing in yourself, not a racehorse, a promising stock or a lottery ticket. The risk should be based on research into your own needs and values.

Going from an abusive lover to a potentially abusive lover is not an intelligent risk; the intelligent risk is trying to make it on your own. Leaving a small town where you've been labeled a queer to a city where you might find yourself is not a risk. It's self-preservation.

Leaving a secure job or career that you find frustrating or boring to try something that you find exciting may sound like a tremendous risk, but if you cannot find joy in your work, you are cheating yourself of the natural bliss which is your birthright. Spending half your life in sacrifice to collect possessions for the other half is ritual suicide.

Life is supposed to be an adventure. If we take control, it will be what we make it. If we do not, we have no one to blame but ourselves.

We are gay because that is the way we are. But if we are to find authenticity and actualization as a human being we must expend effort discovering, developing and being one of a kind—nurturing that strange little plant that is our unique self.

As Anthony, the Unitarian minister, advises: "Pay attention to who you are. Sort out the voices inside your head. Those that would undermine your self-worth are frauds; let them go. Learn to love and trust yourself. The powers you need are all inside of you."

Each morning, I awake—a hundred men and a God.
We walk through the week's seven fingers
. . . into a thousand lives.

For we are one—
I am my sisters
And thee, my brothers

We thank the Universe to be alive;
We thank the Universe to be gay;
We thank the Universe to be me.

My life has become the Sabbath,
For I have touched the world
And I know that it is good.

. . . and this is just the beginning.

Appendix

How Happy Are You ?

The following test of well-being has been adapted from one validated on a large cross-section of the general population. It has been shortened and modified to remove bias for age, and sexual preference. Test scoring and evaluation are on the next page.

Select one answer per question:

1. How often do you find satisfaction in your work or primary activity?
    a. most of the time   b. occasionally   c. rarely

2. Does your work or primary activity benefit society?
    a. definitely yes b. most of the time c. occasionally d. rarely

3. Do you ever feel bored?
    a. rarely   b. occasionally   c. most of the time

4. How responsible do you feel for the way your life has worked out?
    a. very responsible   b. somewhat responsible
          c. not very responsible

(Continues on next page)

How pleased are you with:

5. Your health?
   a. pleased   b. mostly satisfied   c. mixed feelings   d. dissatisfied

6. Your love relationship(s)?
   a. pleased   b. mostly satisfied   c. mixed feelings   d. dissatisfied

7. Your degree of recognition, success?
   a. pleased   b. mostly satisfied   c. mixed feelings   d. dissatisfied

8. Your personal growth and development?
   a. pleased   b. mostly satisfied   c. mixed feelings   d. dissatisfied

9. Your friends and social life?
   a. pleased   b. mostly satisfied   c. mixed feelings   d. dissatisfied

10. The degree to which your life contributes to others?
    a. pleased   b. mostly satisfied   c. mixed feelings   d. dissatisfied

11. Your life as a whole?
    a. pleased   b. mostly satisfied   c. mixed feelings   d. dissatisfied

12. Your financial situation?
    a. pleased   b. mostly satisfied   c. mixed feelings   d. dissatisfied

13. Your exercise and physical recreation?
    a. pleased   b. mostly satisfied   c. mixed feelings   d. dissatisfied

14. Your religious or spiritual life?
    a. pleased   b. mostly satisfied   c. mixed feelings   d. dissatisfied

Appendix: How Happy Are You?

15. Your sex life?
    a. pleased   b. mostly satisfied   c. mixed feelings   d. dissatisfied

16. Your physical attractiveness?
    a. pleased   b. mostly satisfied   c. mixed feelings   d. dissatisfied

17. The balance of your time between work, leisure, home, etc.?
    a. pleased   b. mostly satisfied   c. mixed feelings   d. dissatisfied

How Happy Are You ?

Test Scoring & Evaluation

Add the number of A's you answered to the 17 questions.

If you selected less than 8 A's, it would suggest that you are of less than average well-being.

If you selected 8 to 10 A's, it would suggest that you are of average well-being.

If you selected 11 to 13 A's, it would suggest that you are of high well-being.

If you selected 14 or more A's, it would suggest you are of unusually high well-being.

On a somewhat more elaborate version of this test, people interviewed in this book achieved scores equivalent to 11 or above.

Notes

Chapter 1. The Psychology of Being

1 George Weinberg, *Society and the Healthy Homosexual* (New York: St. Martin's Press, 1972), p. 71.

2 Rollo May, *Man's Search For Himself* (New York: W.W. Norton & Co., 1953), p. 95.

3 Erich Fromm, *The Art of Loving* (New York: Harper and Row, 1956).

4 From column in 1960s, confirmed as still current by Ann Landers in letter to author.

5 May, *op. cit.*, p.96.

6 Abraham Maslow, *Motivation and Personality* (New York:Harper & Bros., 1954), pp. 214-215.

7 Gail Sheehy, *Pathfinders* (New York: Wm. Morrow & Co., 1981).

Chapter 2. Lesbian/Gay Lifestyles

1 C.A. Tripp, *The Homosexual Matrix* (New York: McGraw-Hill, 1975), pp. 127-8.

2 Marie-Louise von Franz, *Puer Aeternus* (Santa Monica: Sigo Press, 1981).

3 Ruth Baetz, *Lesbian Crossroads* (New York: Wm. Morrow & Co., 1980), pp. 17-18.

Chapter 4. Spiritual Paths

1 Betty Berzon & Robert Leighton, eds., *Positively Gay* (Berkeley, CA: Celestial Arts, 1979), pp. 58-59.

2 William James, *The Varieties of Religious Experience* (New York: Longmans, Green & Co., 1902).

3 C.G. Jung et al, *Man and His Symbols* (New York: Doubleday, 1964).

4 Elaine Pagels, *The Gnostic Gospels* (New York: Random House, 1979).

5 John Boswell, *Christianity, Social Tolerance and Homosexuality* (Chicago: Univ. of Chicago, 1980).

6 Peter Larkin, *The Divine Androgyne* (San Diego: Sanctuary Publications, 1980). Available through Alamo Square Press, $25; acknowledge that you are over 21 and will not be offended by receiving sexually explicit material through the mail.

7 Arthur Evans, *Witchcraft and the Gay Counterculture* (Boston: Fag Rag Books, 1978).

8 Richard M. Bucke, M.D., *Cosmic Consciousness* (New York: E.P. Dutton, 1951).

9 The Tayu Order, P.O.Box 11554, Santa Rosa, CA 95406

10 Jane Roberts, *The Seth Material* (New York: Prentice-Hall, 1970). The title of the first best selling book is used as a label for the entire series. It is interesting to note that Seth explains that homosexual activity is just as natural as heterosexual, and that gay relationships are just as healthy. He goes on to say that the preferred state would be bisexuality—sexual love unrestricted by gender. *The Nature of the Psyche: Its Human Expression*, a Seth Book by Jane Roberts (New York: Prentice-Hall, 1979), Ch. 4.

11 Isis is the mother goddess of the ancient Egyptians.

12 Shirley MacLaine, *Out on a Limb* (New York: Bantam, 1983).

Chapter 5. Developing Your Unique Self

1 Joseph Campbell, *The Power of Myth* (New York: Doubleday, 1988), p. 120.

2 Sidney Simon, et al, *Values Clarification: A Handbook of Practical Strategies* (New York: Hart, 1972).

3 Wayne W. Dyer, *Your Erroneous Zones* (New York: Funk & Wagnalls, 1976).

4 Eugene T. Gendlin, Ph.D., *Focusing* (New York: Everest House, 1978).

5 Terry Cole-Whittaker, *What You Think of Me is None of My Business*, (La Jolla, CA: Oak Tree, 1979).

6 Lawrence LeShan, *How to Meditate* (Boston: Little, Brown & Co., 1974), p. 29.

7 Shakti Gawain, *Creative Visualization* (Mill Valley, CA: Whatever Publishing, 1978).

8 Dr. Marny Hall, *The Lavender Couch: A Consumer's Guide to Psychotherapy for Lesbians and Gay Men* (Boston: Alyson, 1985).

9 *A Course in Miracles* (Tiburon, CA: Foundation for Inner Peace, 1975).

For Further Reading

Chapter 1. The Psychology of Being

Fromm, Erich. *The Art of Loving.* New York: Harper and Row, 1956.

Maslow, Abraham. *Motivation and Personality.* New York: Harper and Bros., 1954.

May, Rollo. *Man's Search for Himself.* New York: W.W. Norton & Co., 1953.

Sheehy, Gail. *Pathfinders.* New York: Wm. Morrow & Co., 1981.

Weinberg, George. *Society and the Healthy Homosexual.* New York: St. Martin's Press, 1972.

Chapter 2. Gay/Lesbian Lifestyles

Abbott, Sidney & Love, Barbara. *Sappho Was a Right-On Woman.* New York: Stein & Day, 1972.

Adelman, Marcy, Ph.D., Ed. *Longtime Passing: Lives of Older Lesbians.* Boston: Alyson, 1986.

Berger, Raymond M. *Gay and Gray.* Urbana, IL: Univ. of Ill. Press, 1982.

Clark, Don. *Living Gay.* Berkeley, CA: Celestial Arts, 1979.

Clark, Don. *The New Loving Someone Gay.* Berkeley, CA: Celestial Arts, 1977.

Martin, Del & Lyon, Phyllis. *Lesbian/Woman.* San Francisco: Glide Press, 1972.

Mains, Geoff. *Urban Aboriginal: Celebration of the Leather Lifestyle.* San Francisco: Gay Sunshine Press, 1984.

Tripp, C.A., Ph.D. *The Homosexual Matrix.* New York: McGraw-Hill, 1975.

Wolff, Deborah Coleman. *The Lesbian Community.* Berkeley, CA: Univ. of Cal., 1979.

Chapter 3. Spiritual Paths

Boswell, John. *Christianity, Social Tolerance and Homosexuality.* Chicago: Univ. of Chicago Press, 1980.

Bucke, Richard, MD. *Cosmic Consciousness.* New York: E.P. Dutton, 1951.

Budapest, Z. *The Holy Book of Women's Mysteries.* Susan B. Anthony Coven, P.O Box 11363, Oakland, CA 94611, 1986.

Campbell, Joseph. *The Power of Myth*. New York: Doubleday, 1988.

Ellwood, Robert S. *Alternative Altars: Unconventional and Eastern Spirituality in America*. Chicago: Univ. of Chicago Press, 1979.

Evans, Arthur. *Witchcraft and the Gay Counterculture*. Boston: Fag Rag Books, 1978.

James, William. *Varieties of Religious Experience*. New York: Longmans, Green & Co., 1902.

Jung, C.G. et al. *Man and His Symbols*. New York: Doubleday, 1964.

McNeil, John J., S.J. *The Church and the Homosexual*. Mission, KS: Sheed Andrews & McNeel, 1976.

Pagels, Elaine. *The Gnostic Gospels*. New York: Random House, 1979.

Perry, Troy. *The Lord is My Shepherd, and He Knows I'm Gay*. New York: Bantam, 1972.

Roberts, Jane. *Seth Speaks*. Englewood Cliffs, NJ: Prentice-Hall, 1972.

The Nature of Personal Reality, 1974.

The Nature of the Psyche: Its Human Expression, 1972.

Sizuki, Shunynu. *Zen Mind, Beginner's Mind*. Tokyo: Weatherill Press, 1970.

Thompson, Mark. *Gay Spirit*. New York: St. Martin's Press, 1987.

Chapter 4. Developing Your Unique Self

Dyer, Wayne W. *Your Erroneous Zones*. New York: Funk & Wagnalls, 1976.

Gawain, Shakti. *Creative Visualization*. Mill Valley, CA: Whatever Publishing, 1978.

Gendlin, Eugene T., Ph.D. *Focusing*. New York: Everest House, 1978.

Hall, Dr. Marny. *The Lavender Couch: A Consumer's Guide to Psychotherapy*. Boston: Alyson, 1985.

LeShan, Lawrence. *How to Meditate*. Boston: Little, Brown & Co., 1974.

Simon, Sidney, et al. *Values Clarification*. New York: Hart, 1972.

Bert Herrman, a journalist, is a graduate of the University of Pennsylvania, Wharton School and the Ohio University, Graduate College. In 1990, he resides in the Castro District of San Francisco, where he writes and practices Zen. (Sketch by Ken Gould).